Studies in
Universities and World Affairs—

TRAINING OF SPECIALISTS
IN INTERNATIONAL RELATIONS

TRAINING OF
SPECIALISTS IN
INTERNATIONAL
RELATIONS

C. DALE FULLER

Director, Social Science Foundation,
Chairman, Department of International Relations,
University of Denver

AMERICAN COUNCIL ON EDUCATION · *Washington, D. C.*

*Prepared for the Carnegie Endowment for International Peace
and the Social Science Foundation of the University of Denver;
published by the American Council on Education*

LIBRARY OF CONGRESS CATALOG CARD No. 57-9706
PRINTED IN THE UNITED STATES OF AMERICA

FOREWORD

THIS COMPACT analysis of present-day graduate training available to specialists in the field of international relations is sponsored jointly by the Carnegie Endowment for International Peace and by the Social Science Foundation of the University of Denver. It is an essential volume in the series of Studies on Universities and World Affairs planned by the Endowment in 1953 and now being published for the Endowment by the American Council on Education.

The author, C. Dale Fuller, has been director of the Social Science Foundation since 1953. Among the reasons which made him so logical a choice to conduct this study of graduate training were the following: he had been a teacher of international relations from 1938 to 1953 (with the exception of the customary years in the armed services), he had had firsthand experience in an area-study program designed for specialists, and he had given time to the study of international relations as a discipline. As the volume clearly shows, he has been interested not only from the point of view of the graduate student and of the teacher, but also from the viewpoint of the trained specialist who is utilizing his skills in the various areas of employment.

At first glance the topic seems to be of primary concern to the student who is planning on graduate study in international relations, to those charged with his training, and to those interested in putting him to work after his training has been completed. On second glance, however, the volume should also be of interest to university administrators, to instructors in allied disciplines, and to those concerned with the demand for an ever-increasing supply of competent personnel in the many and varied activities of the international field.

The sponsors can testify to the care with which this analysis has been made and to their satisfaction with the completed study. The author himself is responsible, of course, for the opinions expressed and the conclusions reached in the volume.

JOSEPH E. JOHNSON, President, Carnegie Endowment
for International Peace

S. ARTHUR HENRY, President, Board of Trustees,
Social Science Foundation,
University of Denver

EDITOR'S PREFACE

FEW FORCES have influenced academic institutions in the United States since 1900 as much as the rising concern of the nation with the course and conduct of foreign policy and international relations. The increased importance of world affairs in American life has brought new subjects into the college curriculum, modified existing courses, created new specialist programs in a new "discipline" of international relations, opened new fields of scholarly research, increased the exchange of students across national boundary lines, influenced extracurricular activities, and brought the university new responsibilities in the areas of adult education.

College and university adjustments to the impact of world affairs have been extensive and important to American foreign policy, but they have been rapid, sometimes scattered and uncoordinated, and too frequently unevaluated. There is need for an inventory of what has been done, an appraisal of its value and effectiveness, and a more reasoned planning for the further changes which may lie ahead.

With this situation in mind, the Carnegie Endowment for International Peace launched in 1950 a program for studying "universities and world affairs." In this program the Endowment cooperated with some sixty colleges and universities in the United States and Canada in making surveys and appraisals of their activities and programs related to world affairs. The reports produced by faculty committees in individual institutions were mimeographed for distribution among cooperating groups. Consultative conferences were held. Common problems were identified and experiences assessed. The survey studies were a part of an on-going process of adjustment and development in academic life.

As an outgrowth of the survey program, the Endowment, often in cooperation with other organizations, commissioned a number of specialists to prepare topical volumes dealing with matters of particular importance in this area, to be published by the American Council on Education. The full list of titles in the series is to be found on page ii of this book, the fourth volume to be published. The volumes draw heavily on the survey experiences in cooperating colleges and universities, but are not limited to that experience. They draw on all available resources for the topic treated and involve supplementary research sometimes on an extensive scale.

This volume on *Training of Specialists in International Relations* is presented by the Carnegie Endowment in cooperation with the Social Science Foundation of the University of Denver. In preparing it, C. Dale Fuller, director of the Social Science Foundation, has brought together materials significant to specialists in international relations and to faculties and administrators who have general responsibility for the establishment of university programs academically sound and in the national interest. The volume deals with a field which is of rising importance, and which is a university responsibility in many ways unique to our time.

Howard E. Wilson

May 6, 1957

PREFACE

THIS VOLUME is a description and evaluation of graduate programs in American colleges and universities designed to educate students to function as specialists in international relations. The terms "international relations" and "specialist" are spelled out in detail in the text. Briefly, the former refers to those activities in the intercourse of nation-states which make for war or peace, while the latter is used to designate the person whose graduate training was focused on the study of the relations among nation-states. For example, training in theology and librarianship are not considered herein, even though a graduate of a school of divinity might serve as a foreign missionary and the trained librarian might work for the United States Information Agency in an American library overseas. The former was trained as a minister and the latter as a librarian; neither was educated to become an expert in international relations as such. It is obvious that a great variety of specialists are involved in foreign relations. The training for many careers as they affect world affairs is worthy of careful study, but is not within the scope of the present report.

The type of training dealt with here is concerned exclusively with graduate instruction, that is, M.A. and Ph.D. programs focused on international affairs. Other than academic types of programs, even though specifically in international relations, such as in-service training in the U. S. Department of State's Foreign Service Institute, postdoctoral study, or short courses to orient technicians going abroad to work for the Federal Government, are not considered.

This report considers only graduate instruction because other aspects of the study of international relations in American colleges and universities are discussed in other volumes in the series "Studies in Universities and World Affairs."

The author's observations and interpretations about graduate education in international relations are made on the basis of a survey of the "producer," the "consumer," and the "product." The producer is the university which offers graduate training in international relations. The consumer is any agency—academic, governmental, or other—which employs international relations specialists. The product is the student who received a graduate degree in which he emphasized the study of foreign affairs and who subsequently was employed as an international relations specialist.

The first step in the survey—the analysis of the producer—was an examination of graduate offerings described in college catalogues. Of the 1,855 institutions of higher education in the United States 415 offer the master's degree and 180 the doctorate.[1] Eliminating junior colleges, teachers colleges, technological and theological schools, as well as schools of art, business, law, librarianship, medicine, music, and the like, there remain something less than 200 institutions which offer graduate programs within which specialization in international relations might be appropriate. The catalogues of 184 of these were analyzed.

The weaknesses of a college catalogue are well known. Sometimes course titles have little relation to what is taught. In one large university, for example, three years are required to effect a change in course title in the graduate catalogue, so professors frequently teach what they feel necessary regardless of the label on the course. Many times, on the other hand, programs exist on paper only. A study of catalogues, therefore, does not permit an exact count of institutions offering specialized training in international relations. An estimate of seventy such institutions would not miss the mark by far—approximately thirty-five institutions

[1] Office of Education, U. S. Department of Health, Education, and Welfare, *Education Directory, 1955-1956, Part III: Higher Education* (Washington: Government Printing Office, 1955), p. 8.

offer an M.A. and/or Ph.D. in international relations *per se,* and an additional thirty-five offer the M.A. and/or Ph.D. in political science with major emphasis on international affairs.

To help correct for the inadequacy of a catalogue analysis, problems of graduate instruction in international relations were discussed in some detail with 73 teachers and administrators representing 38 institutions. The detailed self-surveys and appraisals made by American colleges and universities in cooperation with the Carnegie Endowment, between 1952 and 1955, were also drawn upon. The rapidly growing body of literature on the nature of international relations as a field of study was also examined. The great bulk of such books, articles, and monographs was prepared by teachers and researchers in the field.

The author of this report attempts to add a dimension not generally found in other appraisals published thus far, that is, the views of former graduate students now operating as specialists in foreign affairs. This is an analysis of the product rather than the producer. One hundred fifty-two holders of graduate degrees in international relations were communicated with. These 152 persons were asked to evaluate their graduate instruction in light of the positions which they now hold. The method used in this survey of the "product" is described in detail in chapter 4.

In analyzing the "consumer" of specialists, conversations were held with 56 employers, including officers of the Department of State, the Central Intelligence Agency, the United States Information Agency, Radio Free Europe, radio and television networks, nationally known newspaper and news magazine executives and foreign correspondents, representatives of business, officers of private foundations interested in the study of international relations, and university department heads and graduate deans.

It is the author's belief that this examination of the views of graduate instruction held by teachers, employers, and graduates is broader than any previous study of training in this particular field. This survey expands and brings up to date the extremely useful studies of graduate instruction in international relations which have been done earlier in the United States.[2]

This report was written *about* the specialist but not exclusively *for* him. Much of what is contained in it may be known to the international relationist. The individual invested with responsibility for graduate instruction in this field, for example, may gain little but the satisfaction of knowing that many of the difficulties he faces are not uniquely his. However, he may find of use the discussion of how others attempt to solve the problems of graduate instruction.

The report is also for nonexperts: college administrators who frequently ask what the place of international relations should be in the graduate curriculum, teachers in the several social science disciplines who wish to know the relationship of international relations to their particular field, employers who ask what does the international relationist know and what can he do. In the interests of this audience the report is brief, and most of the special terminology of the field—jargon, if you will—has been avoided.

Chapter 1 contains general observations on international relations as a field of graduate instruction—the questions with which it deals, the reasons for the fluid nature of its curriculum, the approaches used in training, and the different ways in which instruction is organized. Chapter 2 defines the "specialist" and examines more specifically the content of instructional programs —what it is that universities feel a specialist in international relations should know. It discusses the skills and personality characteristics desirable for the specialist and describes the career opportunities open to him.

Chapters 1 and 2 generalize about international relations training in American colleges and universities on the basis of the sources surveyed. Not all generalizations apply to any one institu-

[2] Notably, Grayson Kirk, *The Study of International Relations* (New York: Council on Foreign Relations, 1947), and Committee for Advancement of Teaching, American Political Science Association, *Goals for Political Science* (New York: William Sloane Associates, 1951).

tion. Each program in any college has features peculiar to it, and each student enrolling has a background different from others, so his case is a special one. Specific programs of study in a number of different institutions are described in chapter 3 to demonstrate both the individual character of training programs and the general comments made in earlier chapters. Chapter 4 contains evaluations of graduate instruction by some persons who have received such training. The purpose of chapters 3 and 4 is to take the discussion out of the realm of generalization and into specifics. By confining the bulk of illustrative material to those two chapters, it is believed the volume is made more readable for persons unfamiliar with international relations as a field of study. The conclusions which the writer has drawn from this survey are contained in chapter 5.

The writer wishes to thank Ruth Davis, Nancy Good, Miriam Platig, and Inge Schneier for the long hours they devoted to a painstaking analysis of college catalogues. He gratefully acknowledges the assistance of the many persons who in personal discussion and by correspondence have given him the benefit of their thoughts and their experience with the problem of the education of persons to work as specialists in international relations.

CONTENTS

CHAPTER 1

International Relations as a Field of Graduate Study

DURING WORLD WAR II, a young man who had been a college instructor in international relations as a civilian reported to the Pentagon for assignment. He noted the suspicious reaction of the personnel officer to the information about his civilian work. The former teacher did not learn until many months later the reason for the peculiar reception. The personnel officer had mentally placed the adjective "Third" before "International"! The equating of international relations with the Communists' Third International is an extreme situation, but it demonstrates how international relations as a field of study sometimes has been misunderstood.

Recently a high school teacher sent a letter to a Western university. "I have seen the announcement of your graduate fellowships in international relations," she wrote. "Will you please send me application forms as well as information on what international relations is and what one who is trained in it does?"

Again, the illustration is unusual but the question is a common one. It is frequently raised by students, employers, and even by teachers and administrators in higher education. Just what is "this singularly ill-defined field" which a distinguished professor at Harvard writing out of sympathy rather than criticism has described as sprawling "amorphously over so large and varied a domain as to stagger the imagination and place it well beyond the grasp and comprehension of both student and teacher"?[1]

This chapter seeks in several ways to clarify the nature of international relations as a field of graduate education. First, "international relations" is defined by outlining the questions with which the international relations curriculum is concerned. Next, the fluidity of the curriculum is described and the major reasons for this condition are examined. The first two sections of the chapter together show the broad scope of this field of study and its complexity.

The scope and complexity of this area of study have led to erroneous impression about the study of international relations on the part of some persons outside the field. Several such erroneous beliefs are discussed in the third section. The scope and complexity of the field also have resulted in a variety of approaches to training specialists as well as to several ways of organizing graduate instruction in international relations. The approaches to study and types of organization for conducting instruction are described in the last two sections of the chapter.

What Is "International Relations"?

A one-sentence definition of international relations as a field of study is meaningful only to someone well acquainted with the field. For the person who is not familiar with the field, international relations is best understood by examining the questions with which this field of study deals. In most institutions of higher education in the United States, the courses for a candidate for a graduate degree in international relations are selected to develop an understanding of three major questions: (1) *What* do states want which leads them to project themselves beyond their borders? (2) *How* do they attempt to achieve their objectives in foreign affairs? (3) *Why* do they succeed or fail in the quest?

The curriculum seeks an understanding of the three questions

[1] Rupert Emerson reviewing Quincy Wright's *The Study of International Relations*, in the *American Political Science Review*, March 1956, pp. 216–18.

—what, how, and why—in the materials of many disciplines and in a study of past events in world politics. To date, little if any progress has been made in developing methods which will enable specialists to predict accurately the future behavior of states, but present training attempts to produce experts who can provide educated estimates rather than glib guesses with respect to such behavior.

The first question—*What* do states want which leads them to project themselves beyond their own borders?—is a difficult one. The student seeks an understanding of the question by learning to analyze the official pronouncements of statesmen and weigh unofficial sources such as the press, radio, movies, as well as books and articles by academicians. He also attempts to assess a state's aims from its history, its strategic position, the resources of the nation and what it does with them. He seeks insight from the internal situation of a country. A nation's ideology is an especially fruitful source of study. Does the state wish to extend its way of life to other countries? Does it seek raw materials, markets, an outlet for excess population, revenge, prestige? What does a state believe it must do abroad to secure itself against attack and to promote the general well-being of its citizens?

The second major question in the study of international relations is: *How* do states achieve their international objectives? The methods dealt with in graduate study generally are five: (1) diplomacy; (2) propaganda; (3) economic inducements and pressures; (4) international organizations and other multilateral arrangements; (5) military threats and war.

A consideration of diplomatic techniques includes study of the organization of the United States Department of State and of foreign offices of other nations and the observing, reporting, and negotiating functions of diplomats and consuls sent abroad to represent the foreign office. The effectiveness of the tools which diplomacy has at its disposal to bring pressure on other governments is analyzed. These devices include recognition and non-recognition, severance of diplomatic relations, expulsion of the official representatives of another state from one's country, and withdrawal from an international conference or organization.

Propaganda is a time-worn, if not honored, tool of statecraft. Once its principal target was the elite of a nation, friendly or otherwise, the members of which were in a position to affect the policy of the nation to which the propaganda was directed. As the use of radio receivers spread throughout the world, propaganda increasingly has been beamed toward the masses as well as the elite. So the study of this device of states now draws on the works of social psychology, concerned with the behavior of groups, and cultural anthropology, concerned with the character of foreign societies. There is growing knowledge of what influences people and why. Such knowledge is today essential to the international relationist if only because psychological warfare is one important element in cold war.

Economic inducements and pressures as methods of achieving a nation's foreign policy objectives illustrate vividly the multidisciplinary understanding required of an international relations specialist. To show how economics and politics are woven together in world affairs, one need only mention some of the ways economic pressures are exerted by a state. Restrictions of United States exports to the Communist countries of Eastern Europe, the denial of a billion-dollar loan to the U.S.S.R., the threat to cut off trade with friendly states if they in turn should trade with Red China, the purchase by state A of commodities which it does not need from state B, to prevent B from selling those items to A's enemy, state C—all these pressures have profound economic and political effects at home and abroad.

The establishment of alliances, international organizations, and other agencies is a fourth general category of activity in which states engage in quest of achievement of their aims abroad. The reasons for alliances, the nature of them, and their consequences are a part of any course in diplomatic history or in international politics, both of which are almost universally included in an international relations training program. The objectives, strengths, and weaknesses of the League of Nations, the United Nations, and a multitude of international organizations past and present, created to deal with interstate problems, also loom large in the curriculum.

Historically, the ultimate weapon at the disposal of a state in achieving its objectives has been war itself. Short of war, there are demonstrations of military power, such as sending the fleet on a world tour, public testing of nuclear weapons, announcing the development of new weapons, mobilizing the nation's defense forces. All these devices and others have been used as foreign policy maneuvers.

The third general question with which the international relationist copes is: *Why do states succeed or fail in the quest of their foreign policy aims?*

Geography is one field of study which sheds some light on the third question. For example, the student learns from a study of geography to use maps critically. The careless use of maps may lead to fallacious political thinking. A case in point is the debate in Congress in 1867 relative to the purchase of Alaska. Many argued against the purchase because "Alaska leads only to the North Pole." This kind of logic resulted from an image of the world as depicted by a Mercator projection which places the North Pole at the top of the map, at the top of the world so to speak, with nothing above it and everything below it. An opposite and equally misleading image of the world could be drawn from a study of a north polar projection which puts the North Pole at the center of everything on the map.

The geographic position of a state may condition the thinking of its leaders and its people. For example, the United States was isolationist in outlook when it viewed the Atlantic and Pacific Oceans as barriers to attack, but when the realization developed in this country that oceans are also highways which other states might use to attack us, our viewpoint became more internationalist.

The study of geography provides insights about international affairs beyond the effect which the geographic position of a state may have on the outlook of its people, since the geographic position of a state may also determine its strategical opportunities for action. For example, during the nineteeneth century, when all the world's powerful nations were located in Europe and submarines and airplanes were nonexistent, Great Britain commanded the seven seas because she could blockade all Europe's entries to the oceans—the Suez Canal, the Straits of Gibraltar, the English Channel, and the North Sea.

The student must also understand the physical bases of a state's power, its resources of food, industrial raw materials, and inanimate energy. No nation can long remain an influential power in the world without access to supplies for food and clothing for its people and minerals and energy to maintain and develop its industrial establishment. It must be able to protect these resources in war and peace.

Closely related to the quantity of a nation's natural resources is the size and quality of its population. What are the factors affecting the birth and death rates in a state? What is the health of its people? How high is its literacy? What is the degree of its moral stamina? What percentage of the population is in the age group most effective for military service? International relations asks all these questions and others in its attempt to assess a nation's power.

Even though it is a social science, international relations is interested in the influence of the physical sciences and technology on state power. For example, the invention of the steam engine made the textile industry and steamships possible—two very important factors in the creation of the British Empire. An equally significant invention, the internal combustion engine, usable in submarines and airplanes, made it possible for enemy nations to endanger seriously the very existence of the British Empire. Technical developments in the instruments of communication—cheap printing, radios, movies, television—have enormously increased the ability of leaders to influence the thinking of masses of people. The increase in the fire-power and mobility of weapons has, of course, had profound implications for world politics. The influence of science and technology on international affairs must be constantly evaluated in light of the developments in the field of nuclear energy.

Economics is another academic field which contributes to an understanding of world affairs because knowledge of a state's economic institutions is an essential part of appraising its capability. Is a capitalist economic system inherently more efficient than a socialistic or Communist one? How effective is each of these structures in bringing raw materials, tools, and workers together at the right time, in the best place, in the proper amount, to secure quality production of goods in quantity? How successful are the economic institutions of a nation in inciting its workers and managers to produce, to plan well, to save, to exercise initiative?

The international relationist must ask similar questions about a state's political institutions through the study of political science. Are dictatorships necessarily aggressive and expansionist? Is policy formation in a democratic government too slow because all policy must be debated at length in the national legislature and in the press? Is a democracy less able to carry on secret intelligence work? Is it restricted in selecting the best alternative when making a foreign policy decision because of the interference of special interests and pressure groups? How influential is public opinion in the decision-making process?

The disciplines of sociology and anthropology also contribute to an understanding of foreign affairs by the light they shed on many relevant questions about the social structure of a state. What is a society's attitude toward having women and racial minorities in the armed forces and in industry? What does it do to discover, train, and utilize the special talents of its people? What is the morale and discipline of a people which enable it to endure varying degrees and kinds of strain? What are the patterns of family and social relations within a nation that may give clues to the national behavior of the people? What is the attitude toward the state and its leaders? Wrong answers to some of these questions were partially responsible for Hitler's miscalculation of the reaction of the Russians when he invaded the U.S.S.R. in June 1941. Right answers helped the Allies to deal properly with the Emperor in Japan following World War II.

A state's capability for achieving its foreign objectives is determined by its geographic position, its food, raw material, and human resources, its level of science and technology, its ideology, its economic, political, and social institutions, and by its association with other states which share enough of its objectives to ensure cooperative relations. All these matters are relative, however. A state is powerful insofar as its inventory is better than that of its potential enemies. Also, a state's actions are modified by its view of international law and its concept of morality, both of which help to determine when it will exercise its power and for what purposes.

The kinds of questions outlined must be asked not about one state alone, but about many states. Further, the international relationist must study the environment in which the relations among many states take place. The environment of international society is fundamentally different from that of a national society, since in the former there is no central authority possessing a legal and usually an actual monopoly of force.[2]

The graduate curriculum in international relations does not pretend to provide specific answers to the many question outlined. It seeks rather to give the student enough understanding of the meaning of those questions and their interrelationships so that he in turn will be able to ask all the relevant questions about any given problem of foreign policy. It attempts to familiarize him sufficiently with the methods and materials of enough dis-

[2] The foregoing description of the questions with which international relations is concerned draws heavily on the writing and teaching of Harold Sprout of Princeton University, though his formulation has been greatly truncated and somewhat modified as presented here. Other scholars have also developed conceptual frameworks for the study of international relations. The various schemes differ in organization, emphasis, and in details but not in broadest outline.

ciplines—history, political science, geography, economics, and so on—so that he will know where to turn for various segments of the answers to questions. It tries to teach him how to weigh the partial answers thus obtained, and what value he should place on each partial answer in relation to other parts.

This objective is contrary to the general trend in graduate education. The response of graduate training to the increasingly complex problems in all areas of life has been to divide a problem and teach the student all about a portion of it. Fragmentation is one valid and necessary approach, but there still remains the need for persons equipped to pull the parts together. The goal of training in international relations is to teach the student to effect this synthesis with respect to questions of foreign policy.

The Fluid Nature of the Field

The preceding outline of questions with which the study of international relations is concerned shows the vast scope of the field. The breadth of materials to be covered has led to a variety of approaches to the problem of preparing a student to become an expert in international relations and has resulted in a diversity of training programs in American colleges and universities. International relations as a field of graduate study does not have fixed boundaries with crystallized methods and content. The content of curricula differs from institution to institution, and the curriculum in any one university may change rather frequently as "producers" of specialists seek to improve their efforts to educate persons to be knowledgeable in so broad a field. The diversity and change in training programs are described in detail in chapters 2 and 3.

The fluid state of graduate instruction in international relations is not the result alone of the fact that the scope of the field is so vast. The major additional reasons for its fluidity are its youth, the complexity of the problems with which it deals, the rapid increase in relevant knowledge, and the interlocking scientific-philosophical character of its questions. These reasons must be examined if the nature of international relations as a field of graduate study is to be understood.

First, it is a young field, suffering all the growing pains of any infant discipline. Wars are an ancient instrument, and the search for peace dates almost from the beginning of man. The nation-state is a much newer development, but intercourse among sovereign states has been going on for at least three hundred years. Nevertheless, the formal study of international relations in this country is in its infancy partly for the reason that only recently have circumstances forced the United States to have a major interest in foreign affairs. The United States became a leading actor on the world stage about the time of the First World War, but refused to accept the role completely or with enthusiasm. World War II and its aftermath have compelled her to play the part which she rejected in 1920.

American education responded to America's new place in the world in much the same way as America itself—hesitatingly and reluctantly. An occasional organized study program in international relations appeared. George Washington University established a School of Comparative Jurisprudence and Diplomacy in 1898. Two students of Professor Carlton J. H. Hayes at Columbia University during the period 1914–17, though being trained as historians, decided to devote their major work to a study of foreign affairs. One, Parker T. Moon, later became a distinguished professor of international relations; the other, Edward Mead Earle, was a frequent adviser to government on problems of foreign and military policy. A School of Foreign Service came into being at Georgetown University in 1919, and a School of International Relations, at the University of Southern California in 1924. Several departments of international relations were organized in the 1920's and a School of Public and International Affairs at Princeton University was founded in 1930. The Fletcher School of Law and Diplomacy of Tufts University opened in 1933. Individual courses in international relations grew rapidly, and by

1930 most universities had one or more courses which would come under the international relations umbrella.

Political science, the discipline with which international relations is at present most closely allied in most university structures, is itself not an old field of study. About seventy years ago, lawyers interested in public law, historians principally concerned with political history, and philosophers who concentrated on political philosophy pooled their efforts in a common concern with government to create the now accepted discipline, political science.[3]

It is understandable that any new field of study would not as yet have fixed boundaries. In this early stage of development numerous approaches to training are inevitable and desirable. Better insights into problems of world affairs than now exist may well be found in approaches yet to be discovered.

A second reason for fluidity in international relations training programs is the complex nature of the problems with which this field of study deals. Minor problems of foreign policy have interlocking features affecting numerous nations and interests; major problems have world-wide ramifications. A relatively simple decision on the part of the United States to make a gift of wheat to India to alleviate a famine affects not only the Kansas wheat farmer and the citizen of India, but is of concern to friendly nations who may feel we are attempting to take over their markets. It may also stimulate new foreign policy moves on the part of unfriendly states which are attempting to woo India. It will most certainly create considerable debate in Congress and in the press as to what America's policy should be toward countries which are neutral in the cold war. Furthermore, the decision once made is not forgotten by any one of the many parties which might feel that its interests were adversely affected. Developments and actions for decades to come may be influenced for better or for worse by any decision made today.

Should we aid India with wheat? The economist can tell us

[3] Anna Haddow, *Political Science in American Colleges and Universities, 1636-1900* (New York: Appleton Century & Co., 1939); Dwight Waldo, *Political Science in the United States of America* (Paris: Unesco, 1956).

something about the economic effects of the decision in Kansas. The political scientist can shed light on how the action will affect the chances of certain congressmen for re-election. The anthropologist is helpful in predicting the effect on the Indian who receives the wheat. The historian, by marshaling information on United States–Indian relations up to the time of the gift, can give us reasonable grounds for speculating about its meaning for the future. The goal of training in international relations is to provide a specialist capable of combining and synthesizing the conclusions of subject-matter experts and many others in the process of answering the question: "Should we aid India with wheat?"

The complexity of the problems of international affairs is further aggravated by the world-wide revolution which is penetrating far below the political and economic surface of life into the cultural and social depths of nearly every society on the globe. To the revolutionary developments in the political, economic, cultural, and social areas, must be added those in physics and biology.

The H-bomb and germ warfare, as examples, have a profound influence on the data with which the international relations specialist deals. One does not have to be a student of history, or need to read the daily paper carefully, to know that the world of 1957 differs radically from the world of 1937. This elementary fact increases the difficulties of training a specialist to grapple with problems of foreign affairs and helps to explain the fluidity of the field of study; it is changing along with the rapidly changing material with which it deals.

Closely related to the foregoing is a third reason for the fluidity in specialized training programs in international relations; that is, the rapid increase in reliable knowledge from the other social sciences which offer new insights on world affairs. Progress in psychology, for example, has opened up for the student of international affairs the whole area of how personality factors may influence the decisions of statesmen. The growing body of literature in anthropology has provided new understanding of cultural factors affecting a whole people's attitude toward foreign policy.

New data uncovered by historians, economists, political scientists, and geographic-area experts have contributed to ferment in the study of international relations.

The cult of science in America is another source of difficulty for those vested with the responsibility for education in international relations. The miracles performed by science and technology have resulted in a widespread belief in our country—to which many academicians are not immune—that the scientific method can solve all problems. Viewed broadly, science is able to answer questions about phenomena which lend themselves to investigation. Many of the data with which international relations deals are objective, quantitative, and measurable, such as the coal and iron resources available to a state for the purposes of waging war, and the number of persons of military age who can serve in the armed forces. On the other hand, most foreign policy problems also involve basic questions of right and wrong. Is democracy superior to communism? Does might make right in world affairs? Should a nation be too proud to fight? Is it ethical to harm the watchmaker in Switzerland economically by placing a tariff on Swiss watches in order to protect persons engaged in the same occupation in the United States? Such questions of value cannot be answered by the scientific method alone.

International relations study can and must use both the scientific and philosophical methods. The substantial efforts now under way to make as much of the study scientific as possible, and the rigorous philosophical discussions in which international relations experts are necessarily engaged are evidence of healthy intellectual activity in a changing field.

These then are the principal reasons for the fluid state of international relations training today: the vast scope of the field of study, its youth, the complexity of the problems with which it deals, the rapid increase and change in available, relevant knowledge, and the interlocking scientific-philosophical nature of its questions.

International relations is both a broad and fluid field of study.

Before considering the efforts of the "producers" of specialists to make this complex area a manageable one for graduate instruction, it will assist in the clarification of the nature of the field to pause for a look at what the study of international relations *is not*.

What International Relations Is Not

There are persons, primarily outside college and university circles, who have erroneous impressions about the nature of international relations as a field of graduate study. Several incorrect views are sufficiently widespread to warrant mention. One erroneous belief is that the fundamental purpose of the study of international relations is to promote world brotherhood. Another mistaken view regards international relations and geopolitics as synonymous. A third wrong impression equates international relations with area studies.

The first of these erroneous beliefs is that the primary goal of instruction in international relations is the development in students of a kindly attitude toward people in other lands. Tolerance and sympathy for foreigners is a praiseworthy objective in itself. Some statesmen speak in this sense of the necessity for international understanding, hundreds of private organizations devote effort to promoting it, and social studies courses in elementary and secondary schools frequently attempt to develop in pupils a sense of world brotherhood. Indeed, humanitarianism was the principal concern of some graduate instruction in international relations in the past, particularly during the heyday of the League of Nations. But as a goal of specialized training, it was not without danger. Such training helped produce the naïve specialist in the 1930's who refused to believe the reports of Mussolini's atrocities in Ethiopia. In the late 1940's he was the person who felt that Communist China couldn't be as bad as it was pictured. He was convinced that "if citizens of different countries could just get to know one another, there would be no more war."

This unrealistic approach to the study of world affairs was not

long-lived in graduate instruction for it did not prepare students
to grapple with the problems of the real world of good and evil,
where war is as possible an event as peace. Despite the almost
complete disappearance of an unrealistic approach to the study of
international relations at the graduate level, there are those outside the field who still equate international relations with humanitarianism.

Another source of confusion about the nature of international
relations study arose because some college instructors reacted
against the humanitarian approach and the "do-gooders," as they
labeled them, by moving completely to the opposite end of the
continuum. For these professors, international relations became
the scientific accumulation of knowledge which neglects the human elements in world affairs. It frequently stressed the study of
the balance of power, examined the resources which make a state
strong for war, and analyzed the strategic plans of the wily soldiers
of the past, with a calculated disregard for the small and the weak.
The product of this kind of training was the cynic who scoffs,
"Unesco is the dream of the uninformed man who doesn't know
that power alone prevents or wins wars." The study of world affairs solely as geopolitics proved as unrealistic as the wholly
idealistic approach. It took no account of the culture, ideas, feel-
ings, and ideals which motivate men to shoot guns. It could not
explain, for example, how high national morale can help to over-
power planes and bombs as happened in the Battle of Britain.

There are not many such teachers today, but there are a sufficient number of persons outside the field who think of international relations as geopolitics to create further confusion as to the
nature and purpose of this field of study.

A third confusion results from a rather widespread lack of understanding of the distinction between international relations and
area studies. These two fields are closely related and are an
invaluable adjunct to one another. Each is a multidisciplinary
field of study which deals with affairs abroad. However, an area

study program does not attempt to prepare a student to understand international relations as the field was described at the beginning of this chapter, nor does the product of the international
relations curriculum necessarily possess competence as an area expert. A brief look at the nature and development of area studies
will assist in clarifying the distinction.

Area studies existed in American universities only on a small
scale in the 1930's. Army Specialized Training Programs and Civil
Affairs Training Schools were established at selected colleges during World War II to supply area experts immediately needed for
armies of occupation and military government. This impetus was
given a fillip when the cold war required government officials to
have answers to specific questions about geographic areas of the
world little known to Americans. The development of area
studies in American colleges and universities was largely in response to this need of American foreign policy.

The growth was rapid; by 1956 there were more than eighty
formal graduate programs in forty American colleges and universities dealing with the following areas: Africa (4), Eastern Europe
(6), Far East (18), Latin America (16), Near East (9), Russia (13),
South Asia (4), Southeast Asia (5), Western Europe (6).[4] The ob-
ject of area study programs is to give the graduate student an
understanding of the total way of life of the people of one geographic area as well as a control of the key languages of the area
with which he is concerned. He must understand the patterning
of the culture of the area and have an awareness of how human
values are expressed in it. He must know the stated and unstated

[4] External Research Staff, Office of Intelligence Research, Department of
State, *Area Study Programs in American Universities* (Washington: ERS/OIR/
Department of State, 1956, lithographed), pp. ix-x; Robert B. Hall, *Area
Studies: With Special Reference to Their Implication for Research in the
Social Sciences* (New York: Social Science Research Council, 1947) made no
attempt to compile a national roster but reported on thirteen integrated area
programs in 1946; Wendell C. Bennett, *Area Studies in American Universities*
(New York: Social Science Research Council, 1951) listed twenty-nine such
programs.

assumptions that underlie the culture and the interrelation of the cultural systems, beliefs, and attitudes. To this basic foundation he adds a study of how the people's economic, political, and social behavior are institutionally structured. He learns to view this total structure in the setting of its physical environment and becomes acquainted with the history of the people of the area from remote times to the present.

Area studies, like international relations, are multidisciplinary. The fields on which area programs draw, according to catalogue announcements of such programs, include agronomy, anthropology, art, biology, business, civil engineering, economics, education, folklore, geography, geology, history, international relations, journalism, law, linguistics, literature, philosophy, political science, religion, social psychology, social relations, sociology, and others. Of course, no one university offering formal instruction in area studies incorporates elements from all these fields in its particular program, since no university has that many highly specialized persons on its faculty.

Thanks to the work of the Social Science Research Council and its Committee on World Area Research, there is a fair degree of unanimity as to the criteria for an ideal area studies program. These criteria include: (1) official university recognition of the program, supported by the establishing of an administrative unit to supervise training, (2) adequate library facilities for teaching and research on the area, (3) competent instruction in the principal languages of the area, (4) offerings in at least five pertinent subjects in addition to language instruction, (5) some specific device for integrating the various courses in the curriculum, (6) a going program of scholarly research on the area, and (7) emphasis on the contemporary aspects of the region—sole concern with the history of the area is not sufficient.[5] Still another characteristic of area studies is the recognition that normally training should include actual residence and field experience abroad.

[5] Bennett, *op. cit.*, p. 46.

General practice has been to regard area study as an "added competence" rather than a program of study standing on its own.[6] Only a few universities give a Ph.D. in area studies as such, for example, the Doctor of Philosophy in Latin-American Studies; usually the Ph.D. is earned in political science, literature, languages, or other department, with a minor in the geographic area. Many more institutions give an M.A. in area studies, but a sizable number require the M.A. also to be earned in a department with an area studies emphasis.

The person educated in an area studies training program draws on many disciplines in an effort to understand one geographic area. The foreign policy of the country or countries concerned is only *one* of his many interests. The person educated in an international relations training program draws on many disciplines in an effort to understand the world-wide relations among nation-states; the foreign policies of many countries are his *major* interest.[7] Some of the attempts which have been made in American colleges and universities to combine training in international relations with area studies are described in later chapters.

The goal of graduate instruction in international relations is not to produce an area expert or a geopolitician or a humanitarian; its objective is to train persons capable of analyzing the relations among nation-states as described earlier. Even when one eliminates from consideration the erroneous ideas about the nature of international relations, he is still confronted with an enormous field of study and a changing one. Because the field is so broad and fluid, the training of specialists has been approached in several ways. These approaches are discussed next.

[6] Charles Wagley, *Area Research and Training: A Conference Report on the Study of World Areas* (New York: Social Science Research Council, 1948), p. 50.

[7] For a carefully reasoned, concise analysis of the similarity of difficulties which confront those who conduct graduate instruction in area studies and in international relations, see Hans J. Morgenthau, "Area Studies and the Study of International Relations," *International Social Science Bulletin*, IV (1952), 647–55.

Approaches to Teaching International Relations

The ways in which institutions of higher education have approached the problem of education in international relations may be divided into three groups: (1) the choice of one subject such as diplomatic history, international organization, or international politics as the focal point of general study in the social sciences; (2) the use of current international problems as a method of relating materials from a variety of fields; (3) an eclectic choice of courses from among the many available in the university curriculum, that choice determined by the student's undergraduate background and by his career objectives. All three approaches recognize that the complexity of world affairs requires the student to draw materials from many subject-matter fields.

The first approach, which has been widely used in American universities, places one discipline or subject at the apex of the student's multidisciplinary work. Early in the twentieth century, when international relations as a field of study was in its infancy, the center of this interdisciplinary effort was quite generally diplomatic history. The history of the diplomatic relations among nations—situations which resulted in wars, arrangements made to forestall wars, factors leading to alliances and treaties—is still an important part of the course offerings in graduate work. However, the historical approach tends to emphasize that which is special and different in each international situation. A detailed historical study of Soviet policy in the League of Nations sheds very little light on Soviet behavior in the United Nations because the international situation was so different then from that now. The tendency of historical study to bring out that which is unique in any event did not wholly satisfy the desire of students seeking answers to current and future problems. Although diplomatic history is still an important part of international relations instruction, it is not now the main emphasis in most programs.

Another field which has been widely used as the core of training is the study of international organizations. This was especially

true in the period from 1920 until about 1936. The League of
Nations, the Permanent Court of International Justice, the International Labor Organization, and other institutions which had
been created to deal with the problems arising in world affairs
were the focus of consideration. An examination of international
organizations still has a place in most graduate instruction, but
since the collapse of the League in 1936 very few university programs make it the key consideration.

Increasingly since the late 1930's the study of international
politics has been at the heart of many curricula. The tendency of
political science to dominate in the study of international relations seemed natural, because the original interest of political science was in state and government, and international relations
deals prominently with the relations among states and governments.

International economics or political geography occasionally has
been made the heart of interdisciplinary programs. Such programs are usually designed to train a subject-matter expert in
economics or in geography rather than a specialist in international relations; therefore, they were not examined extensively
in the preparation of this report.

A second approach to international relations in the past was to
place chief emphasis on the study of current world affairs. A
strong motive for many a student choosing study of international
relations as a specialty has been his desire "to do something"
about the world's problems. The importance of what was taking
place on the international stage, plus a great interest on the part
of students, led to the current events approach. The "text" for
international relations courses frequently was the *New York
Times*. This development began in the middle 1920's, but with
the onset of the depression student interest in other than national
problems declined precipitously. However, interest in world affairs revived beginning in the early thirties, as Hirohito, Mussolini, and Hitler pursued their programs of expansion. The charge
of superficiality was frequently leveled at teachers of interna-

tional relations who placed an excessive emphasis on current events. It was claimed that graduates knew a lot about the nature of the world as it existed in their college days, but were ill-equipped to grapple with subsequent problems. International relations as a field for specialized study thus acquired a bad reputation among many social scientists.

In actuality, the current events approach was not as dilettante as its critics believed. Considerable effort was made by those pioneering in the teaching of international relations to explore the historical, economic, and political backgrounds of contemporary happenings, as well as to keep up with the headlines.

Nowhere today are current events the focus of international relations at the graduate level, but current problems are frequently used in seminars and in courses as a method for teaching students to apply more fundamental knowledge and techniques of analysis. The influx of GI's into universities following World War II helped to stimulate the revival of current problems courses in some curricula. The ex-GI's had a keen interest in better understanding their overseas experience, wanting to know why the war had occurred, and if another could be prevented.

The third approach to training specialists in international relations, still widely used, is the eclectic one. The program for each graduate student is essentially tailor-made to build upon his undergraduate training and to fit his career objectives. The typical program often consists of a little of this and a little of that—he is given a taste of many disciplines as each relates to world affairs. The selection of courses is described later in some detail in chapters 2 and 3.

Organization of Graduate Study

Just as there are several general approaches to the study of international relations, so there are several ways in which specialized training in the field is organized. However, the approach to international relations in a given institution does not necessarily dictate the type of organization which it uses to conduct training.

Currently, specialized training in international relations at the graduate level is organized in one of three ways. The student's program is planned and he earns his degree: (1) in one of the departments of an established discipline, principally political science, (2) under the supervision of an interdepartmental committee, (3) in a separate school, institute, or department of international relations.

More than one of these types of organization may exist within the same institution, and usually does in larger universities. The commonplace arrangement is the administration and granting of the M.A. by a special institute or an interdepartmental committee, whereas the Ph.D. in the same school can be earned only in a department.

Numerous reasons are given by university officials for organizing instruction differently at the M.A. and Ph.D. levels. One is that the university may have sufficient staff, library materials, and other resources to confer the M.A. but not for a quality, multidisciplinary doctor's degree. Or, the difference may exist for functional reasons, students preparing for careers in government being admitted as candidates for the M.A. in international relations, while prospective teachers taking the doctorate do so in the department of political science. Still another reason is that many administrators believe international relations is a suitable field of instruction for the master's degree but lacks the academic respectability which should be accorded to the more advanced Ph.D. degree.

This mixture of types of organization of study within one university is not limited to drawing a distinction between the master's and doctoral programs. In some institutions the student has a choice of working for an M.A., a Ph.D., or either, under an interdepartmental committee or special institute on the one hand, or for a degree in the department of political science with special emphasis on international studies on the other.

The organization or organizations utilized in any university are usually the outgrowth of that university's traditions and its internal conditions and structure. Sometimes the type of organization is selected not for logical reasons but is the result of internal rivalries of a personal nature or struggles for a larger slice of the university's budget. These factors loom as large within the ivory towers as outside them.

Each method is operating efficiently in some institutions and ineffectively in others. Given some distinguished and dedicated teachers, a few high-calibre students, and an environment of good relationships between teacher and student and between professor and professor, any organization of studies will produce a well-trained graduate. The strengths and weaknesses of each system are not necessarily inherent, as can be seen by an examination of some of the advantages and disadvantages of each type.

Three main advantages are claimed for administration of international relations instruction through a traditional department. First, the standard of scholarship is more apt to be high. This argument was frequently heard in the past when diplomatic history was more widely used than now as the core of international relations training. History, for example, is a discipline of many years' standing, and its departments frequently have rigid standards of scholarly excellence developed over many years. It is also said by some academicians that political science, although a newer discipline than history, has also had more time to establish exacting standards than has international relations. The premise for this argument is that the student's program will have focus and coordination if organized in an established department. This conclusion does not necessarily follow. Departmental offerings may be a bewildering array of courses whose common denominator is so vague as to be meaningless, since they are often a disparate accumulation of years of haphazard choice on the part of individualistic professors with highly specialized interests.

The second advantage claimed for the disciplinary organization is a very practical one: it is easier for a graduate to obtain a satisfactory position if he possesses a degree in an older field. This is particularly true in teaching. Recent recipients of the M.A. or

Ph.D. who choose teaching as a profession spend most of their time giving standard courses such as American Government and Political Theory, and only secondarily in offering specialized courses like International Politics or The United Nations. This factor operates less importantly with employers outside the academic world, but they too better understand what knowledge and skills a trained political scientist, economist, or historian is presumed to possess than when an applicant bears the international relations label.

The third argument for vesting the responsibility for the international relations curriculum in an established department is that the creation of separate departments or institutes tends to splinter and make ineffectual the work of the mother department, political science. This is a matter for serious consideration by college administrators. However, it should be recognized that it is an argument for a broader approach to political science and not an argument for better international relations training programs. It also assumes that the content of study in international relations should be more politics and less interdisciplinary, an assumption with which many disagree.

Two disadvantages of conducting specialized training in international relations within old, established departments were reported to the writer by the graduates of programs which were organized in that way. First, many students regretted the necessity for satisfying general departmental requirements, some of which had little bearing on international relations. For example, a number of persons trained in departments of political science could take only a limited amount of work in international relations because of the time the departments required that students devote to study of state and local government, constitutional law, and such. Second, numerous graduates reported that the departmental interest was paramount in the institutions in which they studied; hence it was difficult to secure desired cross-fertilization with other disciplines.

The interdepartmental committee is another popular device for organizing the graduate curriculum. It came into being as an easy and inexpensive way to conduct multidisciplinary studies. The committee usually consists of a faculty representative from each relevant department—commonly political science, history, economics, and sometimes geography, one of the behavioral disciplines, and/or the modern languages, depending on the university. The most interested representative serves as chairman, usually in addition to his departmental and other duties. Given a dedicated chairman, such a program can have great vitality.

In this survey those specialists who had studied under the committee arrangement were highly critical of it except in those instances where the chairman's prime responsibility was to guide the students working under the auspices of the committee. When that was not the case, students complained that committee members were overburdened with other duties, and had more concern for their departmental majors than for the international relations student. The curriculum usually consists a selection of existing courses from component departments since the committee is dependent on what the separate departments are willing to give for the benefit of the multidisciplinary curriculum. The work is multidisciplinary but often lacks integration. Not infrequently, students report, the representative of any one discipline feels the others to be unnecessary, and no common viewpoint on international relations study exists among the members of the committee.

The separate department, school, or institute is the type of organization least used, primarily because it is the most expensive system of organization. In this survey most persons who regard themselves as international relationists expressed the belief that it is potentially the best system for achieving satisfactory training. A separate entity with its own budget can fill in the gaps in the existing social science courses, and its members have the time and interest to develop the additional special courses necessary. In this way the contribution of many disciplines can be brought together and focused on problems of world affairs. Students particularly like this method of organization since it gives them a "home."

The greatest danger in the separate entity is the tendency to a proliferation of courses which is regarded by many educators as the curse of higher learning.

The differences of opinion in academic circles as to which type of organization is most appropriate for the study of international relations sometimes raises the question: Is international relations a discipline? The discussion surrounding this question has as many facets as there are definitions of a "discipline." If the term means, as it does to many people, a field of study, then international relations is a discipline. On the other hand, if it means a body of data systematized by a distinctive analytical method and capable of permitting predictions with exactitude, then international relations is not a discipline. The prevailing view among persons consulted and sources studied in this survey is that international relations is a distinctive field of study best described as an emerging discipline. It is a point of view, an outlook, a search for answers to questions in a way not now being utilized by the long-established disciplines.

Disciplines are man-made in at least two ways. They may grow out of the systematic thought of one person, as psychoanalysis developed from the theories of Freud, or economics emerged from the analytical endeavors of Adam Smith. Or, they are created, as in the case of political science, by a group of persons bending their efforts to the examination of questions not being adequately explored within older frameworks of study. In either of these processes knowledge may eventually be systematized, college departments established, degrees in the field given, professional groups organized, and professional journals published. All these developments which are regarded by many academicians as the evidence of a discipline are occurring in connection with the organized study of international relations. It is today emerging as a discipline just as political science did before it.

Summary

The goal of graduate instruction in international relations in most American colleges and universities today is to develop in a degree candidate an understanding of three questions: (1) What do states want which leads them to project themselves beyond their borders? (2) How do states attempt to achieve their objectives in foreign affairs? (3) Why do they succeed or fail in the quest? The understanding of these questions is sought by attempting to familiarize the student with the methods and materials of several disciplines. The purpose of training is not to produce a humanitarian, a geopolitician, or an expert on a single geographic area; rather it is to educate a student to understand the relations among nation-states.

International relations as a field of study does not have fixed boundaries and crystallized content. The field of study is fluid because of its youth, the complexity of the problems with which it deals, the rapid increase of relevant knowledge, and because of the interlocking scientific-philosophical nature of its questions.

The scope and fluidity of the subject matter of international relations have led to a variety of approaches to the problem of graduate education in this field and to several systems for organizing such instruction. The approaches to training can be labeled "disciplinary," "current events," and "eclectic." The most widespread types of organization for conducting training are the traditional department, the interdepartmental committee, and the special institute, school, or department of international relations.

This chapter has attempted to clarify the general nature of international relations as a field of graduate study. Since the purpose of study in this field is to prepare a person to become a specialist in international relations, the next chapter spells out more specifically what the specialist is, what he should know, what personality characteristics and skills he should possess, and what careers he pursues.

CHAPTER 2

The Specialist in International Relations

THE VAST SCOPE of international relations study as described in the preceding chapter raises the question: How is it possible to educate someone to be knowledgeable in so complex a field? This chapter attempts to answer that question by defining the term "specialist in international relations" and then by describing how the courses used to prepare a student to be a specialist are selected and integrated within the study program. The discussion in the first four sections of the chapter deals primarily with the transmission of knowledge from professor to student. Since employers who hire specialists evaluate more than the applicant's knowledge, the next section of the chapter describes some of the personality traits which are desirable for the international relationist and lists some skills which it is useful for him to possess. The chapter concludes with a section on the career opportunities for the specialists in international relations.

What is the Specialist?

Comprehending the intercourse of nations as related to the problem of war and peace involves one in a range of subject matter that no degree-granting program can possibly encompass in the one, two, or three years usually allotted to graduate study. Therefore, graduate training in international relations provides the student with a *selection* of materials relating to war and peace.

Depending on the breadth of the materials selected for a student's program, he is trained as a generalist or a specialist. At this point one is confronted with conflicting terminology resulting primarily from the long-continuing debate as to whether a generalist or a specialist is best equipped to serve this country in dealing with foreign policy.

The word generalist is often used to describe those persons who are liberally educated, who know the Bible and Shakespeare, art and architecture, who are at home in the world of quantity, number, and measurement, and who have some understanding of the nature of man and the political, economic, and social institutions which man has developed. The civil servant largely trained in the classics, so highly successful in the British Foreign Office, is cited as proof of the effectiveness of this kind of generalist training for coping with problems of international affairs.

Grouped at the other end of the continuum is a second category of persons often labeled specialists, who also serve their country by handling problems of foreign policy. This group includes, for example, engineers and librarians who assist in the execution of America's technical and information activities overseas. It includes lawyers and economists who use their specialties to handle international legal and economic problems, as well as experts who intimately know the Soviet Union, or Latin America, or some other nation or geographical region.

This distinction between the generalist and specialist is clear. Confusion arises because there is a third group on the continuum located between the two extremes; members of this in-between group are labeled specialists by the generalists, and generalists by the specialists. In this middle group is the kind of expert which international relations curricula in American colleges and universities are trying to produce. The training of these students draws on many disciplines so in that sense they are generalists, but their multidisciplinary study is focused on problems arising among states (the problems of foreign relations) so in that sense they are specialists. An analogy is found in the field of medicine which has become so fragmented that one large medical school now offers a specialization in general practice. That rarity, the family doctor, is now considered a specialist. Similarly, the generalist in international relations is trained in the specialty of looking at a particular problem in world affairs in its entirety.

To avoid confusion in this volume, an arbitrary distinction in terminology is made. "Generalist" is reserved to describe the person in the first-named category, the humanistically trained man. "Subject-matter expert" is used when referring to a person in the third category—the lawyer, economist, historian, geographic-area or other expert. "Specialist" is applied to the in-between category of persons who are broadly trained to use materials from many disciplines in grappling with problems of foreign policy.

The controversy concerning whether the generalist, the specialist, or the subject-matter expert is best equipped to deal with world affairs problems is not as serious as the discussion surrounding it might imply. The intricacy of international affairs requires the services of generalists, specialists, and subject-matter experts alike. There is a necessity for education programs of diverse types.

Further, graduate instruction is only the beginning of a man's professional training. The generalist who enters business, teaching, or government often becomes a subject-matter expert as a result of the assignments he draws in his work. Similarly, the subject-matter expert often advances to top management and policy positions and he becomes a generalist by learning on the job— broadening the area of his knowledge as he moves upward.

Since the production of humanely educated men and women has been the traditional function of training in the liberal arts, a great deal is known about the education of generalists. Knowledge about the training required to produce a competent subject-matter expert is considerable, especially as education has rapidly become departmentalized in the United States. Much less is known about the effective training of the person in between. Graduate instruction in international relations attempts to steer the difficult middle course between training which is universal in application on the one hand and that which is more narrowly restricted to one subject-matter field or one geographic area on the other.

Selection of Graduate Courses

The catalogue of any university contains a plethora of courses which could be incorporated with benefit into the training program for the specialist in international affairs. The major difficulties are those of selection and integration.

A mere handful of schools have international relations curricula in which the student's complete program of study is rather rigidly prescribed, and only about a third of the programs have even a few courses specifically required. The choice of courses included in any student's program is usually an eclectic one based upon the degree candidate's undergraduate background, his career objectives, and his individual interests. The choice is further influenced by the philosophy of education in international relations held by those vested with the responsibility for the international relations curriculum in the institution in which the student is enrolled. Concepts of the most desirable schedule of courses may differ from institution to institution. The choice of courses for a particular student's study program is also affected by the thinking of his adviser about how the student's individual needs are best met. Several study programs are described in chapter 3 to illustrate the individualized character of specialized training in international relations. Nevertheless, allowing for all such special factors, the sources surveyed warrant some generalization as to the core of courses around which training is built.

The student doing graduate work in international relations, whether within a department of political science, under an interdepartmental committee, or in a special school or department of international relations is almost certain to take at least one general course in the field, usually labeled either International Politics or International Relations, as well as one or more courses in

European diplomatic history. It is almost as certain that he will have a course in international organization or the United Nations. If he is studying for the doctor's degree or a two-year M.A., he is equally as certain to study international law and international economics; most one-year programs eliminate the former and many exclude the latter. It is possible but not probable that his program, regardless of its length, will include a course in political or economic geography, but the materials from geography are more apt to be included as a small part of the general course in international relations or international politics. It is even less probable that the advanced-degree holder will have graduate work in any of the behavioral sciences (psychology, sociology, anthropology). To the extent that these materials are included in his program they too find their way into the general course.

Interestingly enough, the persons who were asked in this survey for an evaluation of their graduate training were in almost unanimous agreement that their study programs had provided adequate work in the areas of international politics, international organization, and in diplomatic history. The three areas which graduates reported as having been inadequately stressed were geography, economics, and the behavioral sciences, in that order.

Most universities offer courses in political or economic geography, but students appear content with the amount contained in a general course in international relations and prefer to use their electives for other things, usually more courses in history and political science. Once out of school and on the job, those queried in this survey were almost unanimously of the opinion that if they were to do it again they would seek more work in political or economic geography as a part of their training in international relations.

Almost as frequently the respondents reported lack of adequate training in economics. The economics department of nearly every institution of higher education in the United States offers a course in international economics, or international trade and finance, or international economic problems. Such a course is commonly part of the study program of the graduate student in international relations. The complaint is that too frequently the course is so highly theoretical and technical as to be of little help to the general international relationist. This has been overcome in some institutions by having an economist on the staff of the department or school of international relations, or by having the economics department arrange a special course geared to the needs of the student who is not majoring in economics. A special course of this type deals less with the theories of international trade, income and international balances, exchange rate stability, and alternative monetary standards; it is more descriptive and concerns itself with such things as the reciprocal trade agreements program, the structure and function of international economic organizations, and the economic aspects of assistance to other states and underdeveloped areas.

In addition to an insufficient amount of work in geography and economics, many of the graduates included in the survey reported that the behavioral sciences were inadequately represented in the instruction which they received. The failure of professors to utilize the findings of psychology, sociology, and anthropology to a greater degree in teaching international relations is surprising in view of the increasing effort among researchers to make use of the behavioral sciences in the attempt to understand world affairs. For example, a number of scholars doing research in international affairs are attempting to look behind the structure of states to study the men who run the states. Since the analysis of any foreign policy problem rests on assumptions concerning human behavior, the behavioral sciences can shed light on those assumptions. One international relationist has written:

. . . researches in the behavioral sciences which are least dependent upon historically limited assumptions, especially social psychology, cultural anthropology, and sociology, should be given priority from the point of view of developing a useful science of international relations. This is not to disparage studies in the fields of international politics, international law, international organization, and international economics. They can provide useful guides to policy but the value of a more fundamental approach is suggested by the rapidly changing conditions which may be rendering the assumptions of some of these traditional disciplines obsolete.[1]

The behavioral sciences are producing an ever-growing number of studies which tell us more than we knew heretofore about the general characteristics of human nature, social groups, and social processes. There is a multiplying number of monographs about the elites and bureaucracies of various states, as well as studies of the national character of different countries. Some professors report efforts to utilize such data in courses in international relations. There are also a few institutions in which graduate students of international relations are urged to enroll in courses in the behavioral disciplines as a part of their training. However, the dominant view among teachers of international relations is to regard the data from the behavioral sciences as of doubtful value and of peripheral concern to international relations.

International relations is not the only field concerned with how the behavioral sciences may be applied in a meaningful way to enhance understanding. Witness history, for example, which Toynbee says has been

acquiring a new spiritual dimension, thanks to the pioneer work of Western psychologists within our own lifetime. About twenty-five hundred years ago the Greeks discovered the human intellect; and this discovery was so exciting and so impressive that, from the sixth century B.C. till yesterday we continued to see human nature through the Greek philosophers' spectacles, and therefore continued to be blind to everything in it except its apparently rational surface. In our day, the psychologists have broken through the crust of intellect and have bored their way down, like oil prospectors, deep into the spiritual subsoil; and here they have discovered for us the psyche's unfathomable subconscious abyss. . . . The human psyche is like an iceberg; only a fraction of it emerges above the level of consciousness. Psychology is now beginning to reveal to us the subconscious nine-tenths of the psyche's spiritual depth. . . .

---

[1] Quincy Wright, "Criteria for Judging the Relevance of Researches on the Problems of Peace," *Research for Peace* (Amsterdam: North Holland Publishing Co., 1954), p. 29.

. . . And we can also now begin to see all aspects of human life as so many facets of a unitary human nature, instead of having, like our predecessors, to approach the study of Man departmentally, by breaking it up artificially into a number of separate "disciplines": history, sociology, economics, psychology, theology, and the rest. This new possibility of studying human life as a unit ought to enable us to embark on mental voyages of discovery that have hardly been practicable in the past.[2]

Despite a growing realization of the contributions which the behavioral disciplines can make to the study of social science, a course in one of the behavioral disciplines rarely is a standard feature of the graduate curriculum in international relations. The courses which constitute the core of training in international relations—almost without exception—are international politics, European diplomatic history, and international organization. International economics and international law are less universally included in the basic core of courses, but they are found nevertheless in the majority of curricula.

Beyond the basic core of courses, the candidate for a graduate degree in international relations usually rounds out his program by enrolling for additional courses in history and political science to deepen his understanding of world affairs and to complete the number of class hours required for a graduate degree by the institution in which he is studying. This point is illustrated in the next chapter where are listed the specific courses included in several typical training programs in international relations.

Integration of Courses

Once the degree candidate's courses have been selected, there remains the problem of integrating them in a meaningful way. The term integration, much used and abused, is defined in numerous ways by various people. As used here it means the harmonizing of diverse courses in such a way as to be meaningful to the student in his attempt to understand the problems of inter-

[2] Arnold J. Toynbee, *The New Opportunity for Historians* (Minneapolis: University of Minnesota, 1956), pp. 11–12.

national affairs; it is the relating of materials studied so they have meaning as a whole rather than as a sum of fragmented parts. If difficult to define, it is more difficult to achieve. Elementary and secondary school teachers have been struggling to integrate the social studies for many years. More recently the same attempt has been made at the college level in a variety of general education courses. All these efforts have met with varying degrees of success and failure. It is no discredit to educators in such a new field of study as international relations that they have not found a completely successful method for synthesizing many disciplines in the study of foreign policy problems.

One thing is sure—integration doesn't just happen. Only the most unusual student will comprehend international affairs by exposure to a series of courses touching more or less on world affairs, given in several departments. A course in international economics concerned with balance of payments, exchange rates, and tariffs falls short of developing insights into the nature of economic warfare. A course in political philosophy will provide the student with an understanding of the ideas of Marx, Lenin, and Stalin, but will miss the mark as to how the Communist uses ideology to implement foreign policy. A sequence of excellent courses is a basic requirement of a good curriculum, but something more is needed.

Four principal means have been utilized in the search for integration of subject matter in the study of international relations: (1) the single course specifically designed to integrate subject matter, (2) the cooperative course, (3) the problem seminar, and (4) integrative outside reading and examinations.

Each method serves to integrate multidisciplinary studies to the extent that students have been provided with an adequate conceptual framework for analyzing world relations. If the method used is based on a structure of thought into which the student may fit the ideas drawn from many disciplines, it will serve as an integrator; if no such structure exists, the result is a hodgepodge.

Many of the specialists queried in this survey, who were graduated in the 1930's, criticized their graduate work as lacking coordination and focus. Considerably fewer recent graduates named this as a weakness. This difference is due in large part to the considerable advances made in the construction of schemes for analysis of problems in world affairs.

The most widely used device for integration is the single course, usually labeled International Politics or International Relations. Before World War II, it tended to cover a little geography, a bit of economics, the Covenant of the League of Nations, and current international events, or it was a political history of the nation-state system. Often in more recent years it has been used by instructors to present a conceptual framework for the study of international relations.

Another type of single course used to integrate the subject matter of international relations is the area course. This is frequently a course dealing with the Soviet Union, or Latin America, or the Far East. Its purpose is not to train the student as an area expert, but rather the course is designed as a case study. Its objective is to enable the student to apply his general training in international relations to an area smaller than the world itself. It should be clear from the description of area studies given in the preceding chapter that the international relationist cannot become an area expert by simply crowding one or two courses dealing with a specific country or geographic region into his general international relations training schedule. Area *competence* requires considerable additional study. The use of a single area course as an integrator is not for the purpose of developing competence in the study of an area; its purpose is to explain further the "cosmos" of international relations by illustrating the application of general principles in the "microcosm" of one area.

Cooperative courses are a second way in which integration is attempted. The joint seminar, combining students and faculty from several disciplines, is frequently used. Another variety of cooperative course features an economist lecturing on the economic aspects of international affairs, a geographer on the geographic aspects, and so forth. Still another form is the individual course taught by one person but planned by a group representing several disciplines. One of the most fruitful cooperative approaches is the practice of having faculty members who offer the principal courses in the international relations curriculum all study one another's syllabi and frequently visit one another's classes. Each is then better able to relate his course to the others in the curriculum. This procedure is rarely used in graduate schools for it is a time-consuming process, but wherever it has been tried faculty and students alike praise it highly.

A third method utilized in the attempt to integrate subject matter is the problem seminar. The student draws materials from many disciplines and focuses that information on a single problem—an exercise in integration. To illustrate, since World War II Americans have increasingly urged European states to modify or eliminate the national boundaries which divide them one from another. Congress has officially declared it "to be the policy of the United States to encourage unification of Europe." If European unification were the problem chosen, it would require an assessment of the political, sociological, military, cultural, economic, and other obstacles to unification. The problems course or seminar is a standard device, almost universally included in international relations curricula.

Outside reading coupled with examinations is another method utilized to secure integration. The student is given a list of "great books" which he is expected to read outside his regular course of study. The list varies widely from institution to institution using this device. It usually contains readings of a philosophical or analytical nature which are in themselves somewhat integrative. In addition, examination questions are so framed that the answer must draw on a number of readings rather than from one of the books alone. Titles frequently included are E. H. Carr's *The Twenty Years' Crisis, 1919–1939*,[3] an analysis of interstate rela-

3 Second ed.; New York: St. Martin's Press, 1946.

tions between World Wars I and II which stresses physical might as a principal determinant in international affairs, Erich Fromm's *Escape from Freedom*,[4] a description of German national character from a psychocultural point of view, Hobson's and Lenin's books on imperialism which provide two economic analyses of a phenomenon in international affairs, and some work of Toynbee and of Niebuhr to illustrate respectively a historical and ethical approach to world affairs.

Master's theses and doctoral dissertations are seldom used to achieve integration. Only rarely will an institution permit a degree candidate to select a topic for his major research project which emphasizes primarily the integration of materials from several fields. Most frequently, theses and dissertations in international relations are historical studies; they are focused on a narrowing segment even of an individual discipline.

Each of the methods described—the single integrated course, the cooperative course, the problems seminar, and integrative outside reading and examinations—has utility in stimulating and aiding students to correlate materials from several disciplines. Each gives him a broader, rather than a narrower, view of a field of study which is inherently broad. Each moves down the road leading to consideration of problems in their totality rather than in fragments. Integration, of course, can only take place within an individual. An "integrated curriculum" may still be fragmented for a student so far as his intellectual outlook and processes are concerned. No method now used to help a student achieve an integrated view of the problems of foreign policy can attain anything like complete integration because the theoretical work pertaining to international relations as a field of study is so little advanced.

There is considerable agreement among scholars as to the broad fields in which useful data can be found for the study of international relations, but little agreement as to the relative value to be assigned to various categories of fact, and how they should be

---

[4] New York: Rinehart & Co., 1941.

ordered. A sizable volume on the theories of international relations appeared twenty years ago.[5] Since then much energy has been devoted to the problem of developing theory until today it preoccupies many of the leading scholars in international relations.[6] That agreement in the field of theory is lacking is understandable when one observes that the two disciplines upon which international relations draws most heavily have not achieved the objective. Political science as a discipline has no methodology, fundamental underlying principles, or hypotheses accounting for political behavior to which the majority of political scientists will assent.[7] Historians have almost given up the idea of discovering certain basic laws of historical evolution.[8] Because a widely accepted theoretical basis for systematically investigating, ordering, and understanding data and for hypothesizing about it is lacking, complete integration of subject matter is impossible.

Although universities are struggling with the problem of integration, and rightly so, sufficient progress has been made to satisfy the most recent graduates of international relations training programs, as mentioned above.

Foreign Languages

Knowledge of at least one foreign language is a requirement for a graduate degree in international relations almost without

[5] Frank M. Russell, *Theories of International Relations* (New York: Appleton-Century Co., 1936).

[6] See, for example, the report of a conference sponsored by the Rockefeller Foundation on the problems of theory in international politics. The meeting included some of the foremost scholars in international relations. *Conference on International Politics*, Washington, D. C., May 7-8, 1954 (Mimeographed). The discussions were summarized by Kenneth W. Thompson in "Toward a Theory of International Politics," *American Political Science Review*, September 1955, pp. 743-56.

[7] A report on a conference held at Northwestern University is typical of the current discussion in political science relevant to this problem. Harry Eckstein, "Political Theory and the Study of Politics," *American Political Science Review*, June 1956, pp. 475-87.

[8] See the report on a meeting of historians sponsored by the Social Science Research Council at Princeton University in the autumn of 1953. Richard D. Challener and Maurice Lee, "History and the Social Sciences: The Problem of Communications," *American Historical Review*, January 1956, pp. 331-38.

exception. If the student takes courses to fulfill this requirement, they do not count for credit toward his graduate degree. There is some exception to this practice if in addition to his general study of international relations the candidate is making a concentrated study of a geographic region which requires knowledge of a non-European language. In such cases the student may earn some graduate credit toward his degree for formal language study.

The de-emphasis of modern languages in the public schools following World War I[9] and other factors led a number of colleges to remove the language requirement for bachelor's degrees and some also eliminated foreign language as a requirement for graduate degrees. For the most part, that trend has not been reflected in graduate instruction in international relations.

International relations curricula have retained the foreign language requirement for reasons beyond the traditional one that a scholar should know languages other than his own for purposes of research. There is a very practical consideration for those students preparing for the Foreign Service, since one of four tests to be passed for entering the Service is one in a modern language. Another reason is a widespread belief among international relationists that study of a language, even if mastery is not achieved, assists the student in liberating himself from provincialism. Language is more than a skill. It is a means of understanding the total culture of a people because it is the system through which almost all the activities and beliefs of a society are reflected and transmitted; some knowledge of this tool provides certain understanding of other peoples which can be obtained in no other way. However, the necessity for a knowledge of a foreign language is doubted by some teachers of international relations. For example, one institution which has a language requirement nevertheless stated in the self-survey of its study program:

[9] William R. Parker, "Foreign Languages in Graduate Study," *Journal of Proceedings and Addresses: Fifth Annual Conference of the Association of Graduate Schools*, 1953, pp. 22–33. The percentage of high school students studying modern languages dropped from 40 percent prior to World War I to less than 14 percent just after World War II.

A reading and speaking knowledge of at least one foreign language adds another open window into the world for the student who has this skill. It is no doubt helpful and stimulating to his understanding of other peoples but it is a moot question whether it is actually essential. To an increasing degree materials of other languages are available in good translations and the time to read what is available in English originals or translations is by no means adequate for the serious student. More and more international organizations publish the bulk of their documents in English and almost all international conferences now use simultaneous interpreting so that the listener who understands only English is at no great disadvantage. It is true that many accomplished linguists are quite unaware of the nature of international politics and the problems in world affairs, while some persons who know only one language comprehend quite clearly the vast interplay of forces and factors in modern international relations. Foreign language skills can be useful tools but by themselves they are no certain guarantee of either increased learning or deeper understanding of international relations.[10]

The view that knowledge of a foreign language is not essential to the student of international relations is a minority view, and virtually all programs at the M.A. level require a reading knowledge of any one modern language, and a few specify German or French. All Ph.D. programs and some two-year M.A. programs require a reading knowledge of two foreign languages. Programs requiring two languages are about evenly divided between those which demand French and German, and those which specify French or German plus any other foreign language.

Only a few curricula in international relations require more than a reading knowledge of a foreign language—again with the exceptions of students preparing for the Foreign Service or acquiring an area competence. In such cases, the programs frequently demand in addition varying degrees of skill in writing, speaking, and oral understanding.

The degree of competence in reading a foreign language which is expected is difficult to judge since it varies so widely from institution to institution. Generally, if the student is enrolled in a

10 "The University of Virginia and World Affairs: A Survey Report," *Universities and World Affairs,* Document No. 79 (Mimeographed; New York: Carnegie Endowment for International Peace, 1955), p. 12.

one-year graduate program, he need not demonstrate his ability to read another language until he begins the research for his master's thesis. If he is enrolled in a two-year M.A. program or in a doctoral program, usually he need not show evidence of a reading knowledge of a foreign language until the beginning of his second year of graduate study. Foreign language materials are frequently included in reading lists for courses but are seldom required reading for the course work.

Respondents to the questionnaire who are now engaged in teaching and whose time is devoted mainly to classwork rather than to research felt that the language requirement of their graduate instruction had been sufficient. Instructors with more time for research and persons employed as specialists outside of academic pursuits, particularly those working overseas, found the language requirements for their degrees to be inadequate for their present needs.

Thus far in this chapter, most of the discussion of the education of the specialist has been devoted to the knowledge which a student acquires in his graduate training. The attention which training programs give to factors other than knowledge is considered next.

Personality and Skills

One encounters a startling difference in outlook between "producers" and "consumers" when discussing with each the problems of training specialists in international relations. Teachers preparing students for careers in international relations are primarily concerned with the transmission of knowledge and with the development of skills in research and analysis. The chief interest of employers, on the other hand, seems to be in an applicant's native ability, his range of skills, and his personality. When pressed, some employers will concede that their concern for these other factors assumes first of all that the prospective employee is knowledgeable in his field. However, a surprising number say that the subject of postgraduate study is unimportant. "Give me an intelligent young person who can work with others and knows how to express himself in writing and speaking, and I will take a chance that he will pick up on the job the knowledge he needs."

It is true, of course, that the chairman of the board of directors or the president of a large corporation may speak about the desirability of native talent while his recruiters are at that same moment seeking employees with detailed specifications as to knowledge. The policy-maker in government may discuss the need for persons with capacity for growth, whereas his personnel officer has a particular position to fill demanding explicit knowledge. A graduate dean may deplore narrow specialization, lauding the well-rounded teacher-scholar, but the department chairman may look for a new instructor to teach a particular course requiring highly specialized knowledge. It is also true that the graduate program in international relations now faces difficulty in transmitting the immense amount of knowledge required in the brief time available, let alone taking on the additional burden of developing a wide range of skills. Neither would anyone argue that the teacher of international relations become a therapist to correct the personality problems of his students. Granting all these considerations, the interest of employers in factors other than knowledge is so great that no discussion of professional training is adequate if it neglects such elements as skills and personality. The special attributes for successful duty overseas will provide a useful illustration.

Many of the positions open to the international relationist require service abroad. Virtually any new employee of the U.S. Department of State, since the adoption of the Wriston Committee recommendations, is expected to spend part of his life in foreign posts. A sizable number of employees in other agencies of the Federal Government also work abroad.[11] Jobs in the fields of

---

11 The number of U.S. employees of civilian government agencies abroad as of June 30, 1955 (excluding the Central Intelligence Agency) was as follows:

Department of State 5,603
Foreign Operations Administration 2,510

business or communication also often involve working overseas.

Work abroad is more than a condition of employment. It is a part of the attraction for a great number of students who choose a career in international affairs. Yet most training programs do not take into account the personality factors necessary for successful duty overseas, nor is any serious attempt made to prepare students psychologically for working outside their own country and culture.

Many of the employers queried in this survey stressed the fact that an individual who makes a satisfactory adjustment at home does not necessarily adapt himself easily to a foreign environment. Studies by government agencies and business organizations support this view. One large oil company, for example, considers this matter so important that its employees who are being considered for a foreign assignment are first sent to a center in which the living conditions abroad are duplicated as nearly as possible. The hope is that this experience will reveal any personality characteristics that would militate against the employee's satisfactory adjustment abroad.[12]

U.S. Information Agency	1,143
Department of Commerce	262
Department of Health, Education, and Welfare	195
Department of the Interior	154
Department of Justice	121
Department of Agriculture	105
Treasury Department	100
Department of Labor	60
General Accounting Office	50
General Services Administration	46
Atomic Energy Commission	16
Smithsonian Institution	2
Panama Canal Company	1
Total	10,368

The Representation of the United States Abroad (New York: American Assembly, Graduate School of Business, Columbia University, 1956), p. 14.

[12] M. M. Mandell and S. H. Greenberg, "Selecting Americans for Overseas Employment," *Personnel,* March 1954, p. 359. See also M. M. Mandell, "Working Overseas for the United States Government," *Public Administration Review,* Spring 1954, pp. 125–27. These two articles report the results of a study made of 1,059 overseas civilian employees of the Federal Government.

There is a considerable relationship between an individual's success overseas and his motives for going abroad. Even at the graduate level there are students attracted to a career in international affairs because of what they believe to be its glamour. "Many a youth has been misled by the opera 'Madame Butterfly' into the thought that he might be playing the role of a Pinkerton in a flowering Japan, rather than that of a consul who spends an uninteresting career in filling out papers in some God-forsaken quarter of the globe. It is amazing that more disillusion has not resulted."[13] Like the would-be lawyer who is enamoured of pleading before juries and later discovers that much of the practice of law consists of research in dusty tomes, the prospective international relationist is often unaware that living abroad may involve hardships. The individual who cannot find recreational opportunities other than in commercial sports and plays and television programs may find life abroad very much lacking in glamour. The excitement of travel cannot compensate the individual who isn't happy without American conveniences of plumbing, central heating, and air conditioning. Unless possessed of an abundant spirit of service and motivated by a strong feeling that the job to be done is important, the lot of one who is living overseas may well be a most unhappy one.

Flexibility is an essential personality characteristic for successful work overseas. The person who works abroad for long periods must be able easily to adapt his personal and work habits to a different environment. The rigid personality has difficulty once the novelty of strange food, different customs, and unusual ways of living wears off. He must be able to overcome his love of speed and technology when working with people who dislike change and do not regard progress and efficiency as virtues.

Sensitivity to other peoples is another prerequisite for successful work abroad. This is more than tact, courtesy, and good man-

[13] Woodrow Wilson Foundation Study Group, *United States Foreign Policy, Its Organization and Control* (New York: Columbia University Press, 1952), p. 144.

ners. It means an earnest desire to search for the assumptions and approaches which make another people's way of life different. The worker on a foreign sojourn must be able to divorce himself from the feeling that his ways are the natural ways of thinking and getting along with people. He must understand that his counterpart in another country—the consul, the business executive, or the journalist—may not play the same role in his society that the American plays in the United States.[14]

Another element creating difficulty for the marginal personality is that the American abroad is regarded as a typical representative of his country. His behavior may be the principal means by which those with whom he comes into contact form an image of the United States. He is constantly in a showcase; it is seldom possible for him to dissociate his work life from his private life.

The list of characteristics essential for successful overseas work includes additionally ". . . an interest in and a liking for people, and a healthy curiosity for all that goes on" and "a sound American sense of humor, capable of recognizing and contemplating some of the sorry realities of the world in which we live without being plunged into overly tragic depths of gloom and despair."[15] Good health is extremely important, especially if the duty is in those parts of the world where medical facilities are limited. Some aptitude in "international" sports and games such as tennis, swimming, and bridge is very useful.

Earlier in this chapter, foreign language has been referred to as *knowledge* to be acquired. The international relationist serving overseas must also possess language as a *skill*. Several studies have shown there is a direct correlation between level of language ability and accomplishment on the job overseas. Individuals who are personally dissatisfied with their assignments abroad

[14] The Foreign Service Institute's pamphlet prepared for use in orientation of Americans to overseas living is an excellent discussion of the necessity for sensitivity. *When Americans Live Abroad*, Department of State Publication 6340 (Washington: Government Printing Office, 1955).

[15] George F. Kennan, "The Needs of the Foreign Service," in Joseph E. McLean (ed.), *The Public Service and University Education* (Princeton, N. J.: Princeton University Press, 1949), pp. 98–99.

tend to be those who have no language skill and by reason of this deficiency have become isolated socially from the citizens of the country in which they are stationed. Beyond personal satisfaction, those with language skill have also shown the greatest accomplishment on the job, because they are able to gain the confidence of people abroad and arrive at a more profound understanding of the local situation.

No attempt is made here to set up an inventory of the personality characteristics and skills essential to overseas duty. Rather, the purpose has been to illustrate the importance of such considerations, which in the main are overlooked by the producers of international relations specialists. A variety of informal activities in colleges could be used to provide "laboratory experience" for students planning careers overseas. These activities, including student foreign travel projects, living arrangements in nationality houses and international houses, associations between American students and foreign students on college campuses, are described in detail elsewhere.[16] However, students engaging in such extracurricular and cocurricular activities are largely undergraduates. Little has been done to encourage graduate students to participate in outside activities to supplement their formal training in international relations.

Too often those who are training graduate students for careers in international relations fail to make students aware of the distinctive nature of employment with the Federal Government, whether one is stationed outside or within the United States. Officers in the Department of State and other agencies expressed the opinion during interviews that students recently out of graduate school have little understanding of what a career in the government means as a way of life.

There are many similarities between public and nonpublic employment but there are also differences. Any occupation, of

16 Howard E. Wilson, *American College Life as Education in World Outlook* (Washington: American Council on Education, 1956). See also Cora Du Bois, *Foreign Students and Higher Education in the United States* (Washington: American Council on Education, 1956).

SEE!!!

course, has conditions peculiar to it, but the contrasts between teaching and government—the two major employment outlets for the specialist in international relations—are especially worth noting.

Most government positions require a talent for teamwork, whereas the teacher operates relatively individually. The latter participates in faculty committees, but essentially he organizes his own courses and pursues his own research, governed primarily by his personal interests. The government specialist, on the other hand, frequently copes with problems on a task force basis. He must work with numerous departments, be able to deal with a variety of people, and have considerable skill in reconciling differences in points of view.

Teamwork includes the requirement of ability to accept criticism. Whereas the teacher seldom has his objectives and methods challenged, such questioning is standard procedure in government. The employee at the lower echelons must be prepared for continuous, detailed supervision of his work by superiors. The accountability of those functioning at higher levels is even greater for, in addition, their work may be reviewed by the Congress, the press, and the public.

Still another trait needed in government service is considerable capacity to endure frustration. Because government is so large, there is a degree of emphasis on procedure and routine which the teacher never faces; neither is he confronted with so complicated a hierarchy of authority when he wishes a good idea of his to be considered. It is not an uncommon experience for the civil servant to spend hours of labor on a problem only to have his efforts thwarted when the decision is finally made on the basis of political considerations rather than on the merits of the case.

Another essential quality which government as well as other nonacademic employers frequently mentioned as lacking in employees is the ability to recommend a decision. Some persons interviewed hinted that too much of collegiate instruction, and graduate work in particular, places such emphasis on the neces-

S U . ?

sity for an open mind, the desirability of withholding conclusions until all the facts are in, that many persons with rigorous academic training can never make up their minds. However, the inability to make up one's mind is usually thought of as an unfortunate personality trait rather than as a result of too much schooling. Complex questions of foreign policy urgently in need of answers cannot be postponed until all the background information and facts have been accumulated. The aims sought in the solution of a problem may be mixed, and the alternative courses of action many. Recommending the most promising alternative in these circumstances is an impossibility for the person who makes decisions reluctantly. The teacher does not work under similar pressures.

The expectation that a bureaucrat will be politically neutral is another feature which must be considered, since the politically oriented student is the one most likely to be attracted to international relations as a field of study. Teachers, of course, can be politically active in a variety of ways.

The government employee must also work without public acclaim. If he does a significant piece of research, for example, only a few insiders will know about it. More avenues of recognition are open to the teacher.

This mention of some of the personality characteristics desired in government service as distinguished from teaching is sufficient to reflect the tenor of feeling encountered by the author in interviews with federal officials.

Along with personality factors, those same officials stressed the importance of certain skills, the most important of which is the ability to use the English language as an instrument for clear thinking and fluent but exact communication. This is so basic that one would think no graduate program need be concerned about it, on the presumption that any student qualified to undertake graduate study already possesses it. Unfortunately, professors universally report the presumption to be false.

The most painstaking accumulation of knowledge of foreign

affairs is inadequate preparation for government service if the specialist cannot express himself clearly, concisely, logically, and without benefit of jargon, both orally and in written form. One of the main tasks of a Foreign Service officer, for example, is reporting on the economic, political, and social conditions of the area in which he is stationed. Much of the time of an official at home is spent in drafting memoranda. Skill at written composition is inseparably a part of the diplomatic profession, as is also the ability to speak well. (Teaching + Diplomacy + Grad Student)

The capacity to read rapidly, accurately, and with comprehension is a necessity for men who must deal all their lives with the memoranda written by others as well as with a multitude of other documents. So many officers lack this capacity that the Foreign Service Institute of the U. S. Department of State had to establish reading rate improvement courses designed to increase the reading speed of Foreign Service officers while at the same time maintaining or increasing their level of comprehension.

If graduate programs can provide government with specialists trained to view a diversity of problems in their totality, who possess adequate personalities and are well equipped with basic skills, then government has employees potentially able to move quickly into executive, supervising, and administrative types of duties. It is at this point that still another ability is required—administrative. Talent for directing, training, and evaluating subordinate personnel, and for maintaining a productive and efficient organization is rare, and training devices to develop such talents are scarce.

A key to the importance which government places on knowledge in relation to other factors may be seen in the coverage of the Foreign Service examination, virtually the only road by which the graduate student may enter the Department of State. One part of the written examination is a test of English expression, to determine the candidate's ability to write correctly and effectively, organize his ideas properly, and suit his language to the particular job at hand. Part Two is a test of general ability, that is ability to read, analyze, and interpret data. Part Three is a test of general background, designed to measure the breadth of understanding of the ideas and concepts which are basic in the development of the United States and other countries. It tests the candidate's understanding of the historical past, particularly as it explains the present, and probes his familiarity with forms of government, political practices, major principles of economic theory, and his understanding of the relationships between the different aspects of man's development. Fifty percent of the questions in the general background test deal with the social studies, 25 percent with the humanities, and the remainder with science. The fourth part of the examination is a test in modern language. If the candidate passes these four written examinations, he is then given an oral examination to test reactions to difficult or embarrassing questions, clarity and precision in oral expression, forcefulness, earnestness, initiative, imagination, and versatility.

The successful teacher, as well as the civil servant, must have much more than knowledge of his discipline. For many years there has been widespread criticism that graduate programs in numerous fields of learning are inadequate to prepare students for teaching in those fields.

The study of persons who received the doctorate during the decade of the 1930's, carried out by the Commission on Teacher Education of the American Council on Education, found graduate training left much to be desired as preparation for teaching.[17] A 1954–55 inquiry, conducted under the auspices of the Fund for the Advancement of Education, revealed much the same picture. In the latter study, answers to questionnaires were received from 4,860 persons, mostly teachers holding the doctorate. Fifty percent of those replying declared the graduate program as now generally organized in their fields, which included political science, history, economics, languages, philosophy, philology, and

---

[17] Ernest V. Hollis, *Toward Improving Ph.D. Programs* (Washington: American Council on Education, 1945).

sociology, provided less than adequate preparation for classroom teaching.[18]

Some of the widespread criticism deals with the content of instruction; the fault, overspecialization. Graduate instruction in international relations, as has been pointed out, sins less in this regard than many older fields of study. Much of the complaint about teacher training programs, however, revolves around the failure to obtain candidates for teaching who have "superior personal qualities." Teaching is essentially an expression of personality; for proof, one needs only to reflect on the good and bad instructors he has had. In addition to knowledge of a subject-matter field, the student can learn something about teaching methods and techniques, but these additions will not markedly increase his teaching ability if he has an uninspired, ineffective personality. It is perhaps needless to add that basic skills in reading, writing, and speaking are as essential for the good teacher as for the government servant.

The interest which academic and nonacademic employers place on factors other than knowledge is too often overlooked in international relations training programs. There is little formal attention to personality factors, for example. The conscientious director of studies in international relations who has a light teaching load and is not required to "publish or perish" may take personality factors into account as he advises students on careers and assists them to find positions. Too frequently, however, instructors under the pressure of many duties do not have the time to get to know their students well enough to assess them as whole persons, or are understandably reluctant to deal with personality defects beyond their power of remedying.

Very few programs have an admission policy which recognizes personality factors. Only one program known to the author requires a personal interview of all applicants, one purpose of which

[18] F. W. Strothmann, *The Graduate School Today and Tomorrow* (New York: Fund for the Advancement of Education, 1955), p. 39.

is to evaluate personality. Several programs require letters of recommendation before the candidate is admitted to graduate study, and the recommenders are asked to comment on factors other than knowledge. But general practice is to base admission on scholarship as evidenced by undergraduate grades supplemented perhaps by scores on the Graduate Record Examination.

Concern for skills other than research and analysis varies widely from professor to professor, but examples of curricula which give formal attention to other skills are hard to find. The conscientious professor of course, while deploring what he calls the failure of college or secondary instruction to teach students how to use the English language, will nevertheless take time to correct written work for grammar and style. An occasional professor provides opportunity for his doctoral students who are preparing to teach to lecture to classes in order that the doctoral candidate may gain some teaching experience. Some professors have special sessions for teaching assistants in which the effectiveness of their teaching is discussed. Now and then a college catalogue lists a course with some such title as Problems in the Teaching of Political Science or The Teaching of International Relations, but those that deal with problems other than the subject-matter type are hard to find; most do not consider techniques and skills.

A professor here and there organizes a class project by forming students into committees to give them experience in the teamwork procedure so widely used in government. Most teachers must fight the inclination in this kind of activity to judge its success exclusively on the basis of the knowledge which the student acquires. Many teachers report that committee work is of less value for acquiring knowledge than other, more standard, teaching devices, but the method often develops skills of leadership such as understanding of how to organize a committee, how to set up agenda, how to conduct meetings, and what part to take in discussion. The student may also acquire skills of group membership which include knowing what part to take in discussions, how to draw out other members, how and when to assume temporary leadership, what statements or remarks will improve committee function and which will disrupt the group, how to help the leader handle difficult participants, and other abilities of this nature. The committee method promotes efficiency in oral communication and provides an excellent experience in giving and receiving criticism in a group situation.[19]

The principal way in which most graduate training programs in international relations seek to develop students' skill in research is the writing of the master's thesis and/or the doctoral dissertation. Some programs no longer require a thesis for the M.A., substituting additional hours of course work instead, but these are the minority. Insofar as the writer was able to judge, in most institutions the M.A. thesis is still regarded as a little doctoral dissertation. Quite generally, the student writing either a thesis or dissertation assembles and organizes a mass of data concerning a relatively narrow topic. As an original contribution to knowledge the written work may disclose a few new facts, but for the most part it is devoted to ordering many more facts previously known. Library research techniques are utilized in the main rather than questionnaires, interviews, polling devices, and other techniques. Topics are predominantly historical and draw on the familiar primary and secondary materials of history and political science, seldom venturing into the source materials of other disciplines, even though international relations is a multidisciplinary field of study.

This apparent inconsistency is generally justified by teachers on the grounds that a student should be rigorously disciplined in fact-finding and trained to be cautious in deductions from facts before attempting the more difficult and sophisticated task of

[19] These generalizations are based in the main on the experiences of the Air University and the National War College, which have made considerable use of committee work as a training device. Frank Restle, "Committee Problem-solving Techniques at the National War College," *HumRRO Technical Report 10* (Washington: Human Resources Research Office, George Washington University, 1954); Human Resources Research Office, "Evaluation of Instruction in Staff Action and Decision Making," *Technical Research Report No. 16*, December 1953.

multidisciplinary research. Policy research which attempts to select the best of alternative solutions to a problem, or theoretical research designed to test the validity of a generalization are rarely allowed in doctoral dissertations in international relations. In a number of training programs, seminar papers and term papers in problems courses are used as a means for the student to test his wings in forms of research other than that which is descriptive in depth.

The term "specialist in international relations" has been defined in this chapter and further clarified by a description of the courses which the graduate student takes to prepare himself to be a specialist and by a discussion of some of the personality factors and skills which are desirable for the specialist. The meaning of the term can be further understood by an examination of the nature and number of career opportunities open to the specialist.

Careers for the Specialist

The typical university catalogue indicates that its graduate instruction in international relations is designed for students preparing for careers in teaching, government service, international agencies, international business and commerce, the work of foundations and other private agencies interested in world affairs, and journalism. These many endeavors may give the erroneous impression that the opportunities for a specialist in international relations are limitless. It is true that the incredible increase in the importance of the United States' role in world affairs has opened up a variety of jobs. But the market has been good in part because the output of advanced-degree holders has been small. Only 321 doctor's degrees in international relations were awarded in the thirty-year period from 1926 to 1955.[20] The number of M.A. and Ph.D. degrees in international relations conferred during the past six years is as follows:

[20] Mary Irwin (ed.), *American Universities and Colleges* (7th ed.; Washington: American Council on Education, 1956), p. 69.

Year	M.A.	Ph.D.[21]
1954–55	215	20
1953–54	219	33
1952–53	256	13
1951–52	227	11
1950–51	264	17
1949–50	279	25

Most graduates earning the Ph.D. have become college teachers, the bulk of M.A.'s secured employment with the Federal Government, and a relatively small number of either found employment in other pursuits.[22]

[21] Figures reported by college and university registrars to the U. S. Office of Education and tabulated in *Earned Degrees Conferred by Higher Educational Institutions* for the years indicated (Washington: Government Printing Office).

In addition, an unknown number of degrees reported as political science were awarded persons who had emphasized international relations in their programs. Perhaps some clue as to the number is found in the study conducted by the American Council of Learned Societies under the sponsorship of the Department of Defense in 1952. Replies to questionnaires were received from about one third of the social scientists presumed to be employed professionally in the United States. Among the political scientists replying, 12 percent considered themselves as having a detailed specialty in international relations. *Personnel Resources in the Social Sciences and the Humanities*, U. S. Department of Labor Bulletin No. 1169 (Washington: Government Printing Office, 1954), p. 38.

Another estimate suggests that there are 2,550 full-time college and university teachers of political science as compared with only 150 teachers of international relations. J. F. Wellemeyer, "Full-Time Teachers in American Colleges and Universities," *School and Society*, June 23, 1956, p. 221. A check of the *Directory of the American Political Science Association* reveals that 219 of the association's teaching members list international relations as a teaching field and an additional 281 give international politics, international organization, and foreign relations as specialties. This would indicate that of 2,550 teachers of political science, 500 have at least a subspecialty in international relations.

[22] Other surveys, also very limited as this one has been, support this generalization. The American Council of Learned Societies survey cited in footnote 21, *supra*, found political scientists, including those with specialties in international relations and area study, distributed 46.6 percent in colleges and universities, 31.4 percent in the Federal Government, 1.2 percent in international organizations (p. 88). Another survey covering persons who received the doctorate in the decade of the 1930's and who were employed as of September 1940 disclosed that of those holding the Ph.D. in international relations 60.7 percent were teaching in institutions of higher education, 28.9 percent were engaged in other educational activities, and 10.5 percent were employed in government or business. Cited in American Political Science As-

College teaching, the principal employment of the Ph.D. in international relations in the past, will probably continue to be the chief source of positions. The present shortage of college teachers will become increasingly critical, and many more persons than in the past who hold only the M.A. may be able to use college teaching as a vocational outlet if they so choose. Estimates of the number of college teachers in the United States today vary from 150,000 to 190,000. If one third of the young people of college age in 1970–71 attend an institution of higher learning, a total of 351,587 college teachers will be needed; if 40 percent attend, the number of teachers required will be 453,661; if 50 percent attend, the need will be 555,734.[23]

It is not known what the major fields of interest of the growing number of college students will be. More instructors may be needed in the physical sciences and the humanities than in the social studies. But lacking evidence to the contrary, one may assume the need for teachers of social science, including international relations, will accelerate rapidly. In addition to being equipped to teach international relations *per se,* the specialist trained in this multidisciplinary field is better equipped than most to teach in the increasingly popular general education courses in the social sciences.

One occupational goal of many graduate students in international relations not interested in teaching is the Department of State. The number of positions available there fluctuates with

---

sociation, *Goals for Political Science* (New York: William Sloane Associates, 1951), p. 256. See also a survey of the placement of graduates and former students of twenty-three university area study programs during the period June 1946—February 1953 which covered mostly persons holding the M.A. Occupations of 443 were tabulated: 50 percent were working in government or with international agencies, 30 percent in academic institutions, 12 percent in business, industry, law, and journalism, and 8 percent were employed by foundations or other private organizations. Joseph B. Casagrande and Elbridge Sibley, "Area Research Training Fellowships and Travel Grants for Area Research: An Epilogue," *Social Science Research Council Items,* December 1953, p. 41.

[23] Ronald B. Thompson and Thomas Crane, *The Impending Tidal Wave of Students* (American Association of Collegiate Registrars and Admissions Officers, 1954), p. 34.

the state of world affairs and with the mood of the executive and the Congress. The total personnel of the Department of State, including the Foreign Service, amounted to only 4,726 employees in 1930. By 1950, the number employed directly by the Department had advanced to 26,449. Between 1953 and 1955, during the RIF (reduction in force) and governmental reorganization, State's budget shrank by over one-fourth and hiring of new personnel almost ceased. It is now estimated that between three hundred and five hundred new professional employees will be recruited by the Department annually under the recently revised system of entry.

The Department of State, of course, does not require that candidates for these positions have engaged in graduate studies. Examinations are theoretically geared to the level of academic achievement within the reach of persons holding bachelor's degrees. However, as might be expected, a significantly greater percentage of students who pursued graduate studies and attempted the Foreign Service examination have passed it than those who have done no graduate study. Neither is it surprising that a sizable number of persons holding higher positions have engaged in graduate training. The McCamy and Corradini study of people who occupied policy-making positions in the Department of State in 1951–52 disclosed that 35.8 percent had an M.A. or the equivalent, 13.7 percent a Ph.D., and an additional 23.9 percent had had some graduate instruction but possessed no advanced degree.[24] Also, graduate study may qualify the applicant to enter the Department of State at a higher grade than if he had not engaged in any graduate study.

Careers in other branches of government which interest the international relations specialist are strictly limited. Although the Federal Government employs nearly 2.5 million civilian workers, only 10,000 of these are social scientists. The Commission on

[24] J. L. McCamy and A. Corradini, "The People of the State Department and the Foreign Service," *American Political Science Review,* December 1954, p. 1076.

Organization of the Executive Branch of the Government (the Hoover Commission) in 1949 found over forty different departments and other executive agencies to be directly concerned with aspects of American foreign policy. But civilian overseas jobs with the Departments of the Air Force, Army, and Navy and positions in the Departments of Agriculture, Commerce, and Labor related to foreign affairs are largely for subject-matter experts or are of a clerical or administrative nature. However, the international relationist does on occasion obtain positions in these and other federal agencies.

An international relations specialist, especially if he has good language training and suitable personality characteristics, qualifies well for work with either the Central Intelligence Agency or the United States Information Agency. Statistical information is not available about the number of career opportunities in the CIA, but a large number of the professors of international relations contacted in the survey reported that many of their former graduate students obtained positions in the CIA. The USIA employs approximately 3,000 Americans in Washington and abroad as public affairs officers, cultural affairs officers, information officers, press officers, and the like. International relations is one of the fields of education most suitable for these careers. Most of the openings in USIA, however, are for specialists who have had considerable work experience; approximately fifty appointments are made annually from among recent graduates of institutions of higher education.[25]

There are 29 bodies, agencies, and commissions in the United Nations structure and some 30 regional and multilateral organizations of which the United States is a member and in which the international relations specialist finds positions, but the number of opportunities is restricted. Generally, the composition of each organization's secretariat must include nationals of each member state, often according to some proportional allocation of places;

[25] *Federal Careers: A Directory for College Students* (Washington: Government Printing Office, 1956), p. 35.

therefore, only a limited number of United States citizens may be employed by any one agency. Also, many of the available positions in international organizations are for subject-matter experts.

Importers and exporters and others with international commercial interests, including the fields of banking and transportation, take their employees of United States nationality largely from graduates of schools of business. Most of their overseas staffs are chosen from the citizens of the particular country or countries in which they operate.

There are more than 375 foundations and private organizations in the United States with a major or secondary interest in some aspect of world affairs.[26] Staffs of these agencies are generally small, but persons with graduate training in international relations are welcome applicants for such openings as exist. In this field, as in most nonacademic areas, it must be remembered that skills in organization and administration and often ability of a promotional nature are as essential to the employer as is knowledge about world affairs.

Frequently, international relations majors hope for careers in radio, television, and newspaper and magazine journalism. This is at present only a potential field of employment. The number of foreign correspondents maintained by the mass media is declining, and skill in communication is the *sine qua non* for a position. One widely respected newsman, whose by-line is known to every reader of one of America's papers which gives extensive coverage to foreign affairs, described for this author what he felt was the best way to become a foreign correspondent:

Go to college in a state capital. If you take some international relations courses, that's fine, but the important thing is to get a part-time

[26] Wilmer S. Rich, *American Foundations and Their Fields* (7th ed.; New York: Raymond Rich Associates, 1955); Ruth Savord and Donald Wasson (comp.), *American Agencies Interested in International Affairs* (New York: Council on Foreign Relations, 1955); *American Foundations News* (published in volumes of eight issues each by American Foundations Information Service, New York); *Institutes of International Affairs* (New York: Carnegie Endowment for International Peace, 1953).

job on the local paper reporting events at the state house. Upon graduation bone up on language at Berlitz and then go overseas on your own— it is too expensive for the paper to send you. Pester an American newspaper office abroad or the representative of one of the press services for an assignment. If you get one, make good on it and you may become a foreign correspondent.

This description illustrates another point with respect to employment opportunities; that is, the need to educate prospective employers, academic and nonacademic, to the value of an advanced degree in international relations. Like the poet who was compelled to create in the public a taste for his poetry, the products of this relatively new field of graduate instruction will increase the demand for themselves and others with similar training as they prove themselves on the job. The market for international relations specialists will continue to expand if institutions giving graduate instruction in international relations concentrate their efforts on rigorous training of carefully selected students.

Summary

The term "specialist in international relations" as used in this volume refers to the person who is trained in a graduate program in international relations. He is trained to draw on many disciplines to understand the complex problems of world affairs. He is distinguished from the generalist who is broadly educated in the liberal arts and from the subject-matter expert whose training is more narrowly restricted to one discipline or to one geographic area. Those vested with responsibility for graduate education in international relations believe that the specialist in international relations is a valuable addition to the team of generalists and subject-matter experts—that the international relationist has a view of foreign policy problems which differs from the view of the generalist and the subject-matter expert, and therefore the specialist can contribute something to the understanding of world problems which neither the generalist nor the subject-matter expert can supply.

Persons who have been graduated from international relations study programs are of the opinion that those programs in general provide students who are aiming toward careers in international relations with an adequate background in international politics, diplomatic history, and international organization. The programs are less effective in providing an understanding of geography, economics, and the behavioral sciences as those disciplines relate to the study of world affairs. Graduates of specialized training programs also believe that the programs are more effective in the development of skill in research and analysis than in the development of skill in written and oral communication in English and in foreign languages. Many employers of international relations specialists are also critical of the producers of specialists for failure to devote more effort to the development of a wide range of skills in graduate students. In addition, employers are critical of potential specialists in international relations because often they lack certain personality characteristics deemed desirable for a person planning a career in international relations. Included among the personality traits which employers seek in employees are flexibility, sensitivity to foreigners, curiosity, sense of humor, ability to accept criticism, capacity to endure frustration, and ability to recommend a decision.

The principal vocational outlets for holders of advanced degrees in international relations are teaching and government service. Fewer students trained to be specialists in international relations find work in international agencies, international business and commerce, private agencies which deal with world affairs, and in the field of journalism. However, producers of specialists believe there is a great need for persons equipped with a broad understanding of world affairs in all the occupations named and more. It is reasonable to assume that this need will translate itself into an expanding number of positions open to international relationists to the extent that the present quality of graduate training in international relations is maintained and improved and to the extent that the specialists produced by graduate programs possess not only knowledge but certain desirable personality traits and certain essential skills as well.

CHAPTER 3

Sketches of Some Training Programs

THUS FAR IN this volume, international relations as a field of graduate study has been examined, the term "specialist in international relations" has been defined, and the nature of the curricula designed to train an international relationist has been described. The picture which has been presented in chapters 1 and 2 is the over-all picture of specialized training in international relations at the graduate level in American colleges and universities. The generalizations which were made were based on the sources surveyed during the preparation of this report; those sources are described in detail in the Preface to this volume.

The preceding chapters have dealt with the *general* objectives of graduate instruction in international relations which are broadly similar in most institutions of higher education. However, *specific* objectives of curricula, assumptions as to what constitutes the "best" training, and methods for dealing with the difficulties of multidisciplinary study often differ from institution to institution. Therefore, several training programs will now be described in some detail to demonstrate the similarities and differences in curricula, as well as to illustrate the generalizations made in earlier chapters.

It was pointed out in the Preface that there are approximately seventy colleges and universities in the United States which provide specialized training in international relations. The limitation on the size of this book and the desirability of avoiding undue repetition prohibit a detailed description of all programs now in operation. Therefore only fifteen programs in eleven institutions are outlined. Most of those described below are typical of programs found in many institutions of higher education or they have many aspects which are representative of the kind of academic endeavor now under way. A few of the programs described are not typical ones but they have certain features worth noting for the way they cultivate the knowledge, skills, and personality traits of a specialist. Such factors as the geographical location of a university or whether it is a public or private institution were not considered when selecting the programs to be described since the location and control of an institution do not materially affect the way in which it attempts to train specialists in international relations.

The first section of this chapter describes programs which require a minimum of two years of graduate study and lead to the master's degree in international relations, to the Ph.D. in international relations, or to the Ph.D. in political science with emphasis on international relations. The programs described are those at Columbia University, the Fletcher School of Law and Diplomacy, Princeton University, and Yale University. The second section considers curricula which require a minimum of one year of graduate study. The programs at the Universities of Virginia, Denver, and Connecticut are outlined to illustrate the kind of curriculum which leads to the master's degree in international relations *per se,* and the programs at the Universities of Wisconsin, Florida, and Oregon are cited as examples of curricula leading to the M.A. in political science with emphasis on international relations. The chapter concludes with a description of a program at Western Reserve University in which an unusual attempt is made to develop skills in graduate students.

The Two-Year M.A. and the Ph.D.

COLUMBIA UNIVERSITY

The two-year program for the degree of Master of International Affairs (M.I.A.) given by the School of International Affairs at Columbia University can be used to illustrate a number of comments about graduate instruction in international relations which were made in earlier chapters. The program is an example of a rather rigidly prescribed curriculum, one which is geared to specific career objectives of students, and one which seeks to combine several types of training.

The curriculum of Columbia's School of International Affairs has three objectives in view: to provide the student with a background in general international relations, to develop a functional specialization, and to give him some understanding of one geographic area. In pursuit of these objectives the student must complete sixty semester hours of graduate course work. The sequence of courses differs depending upon whether the student seeks a career in international business, international economics, international governmental relations, international legal affairs, or in international administration.

In order to show more explicitly the nature of the curriculum for the M.I.A., the course of study described below is for a student who hopes for a career in a government agency dealing with international economic problems. The student takes twenty-four semester hours of course work to develop his general background in international relations, eighteen semester hours of course work to develop his functional specialty in economics, and eighteen semester hours of course work to develop his understanding of one geographic area.

The courses designed to enhance the student's understanding of general international relations are all specifically required unless he has had equivalent courses at the undergraduate level. The required general courses are: (1) Basic Factors in World Politics, (2) International Trade and Finance, (3) International Law, (4) International Organization and Administration, (5) Economic Analysis, and (6) a Special Lecture Course on significant problems of contemporary international affairs. The purpose of the six courses is "to give the student some knowledge of the diverse political and economic forces and institutions which have developed in major countries of the world and an understanding of the way in which these forces project themselves beyond national boundaries into the international sphere."[1]

The student must also take five courses to develop his knowledge of international economics; two of these are electives and three are ones which are specified. The specified courses for the functional specialization in economics are: (1) Comparative Economic Organization, (2) Income, Employment, and International Trade, and (3) a Seminar in International Economic Problems.

In addition to six courses in general international relations and five courses in economics, the candidate for the M.I.A. must take several additional courses to familiarize himself with one geographic area. He may elect to concentrate on one of the following areas: Western Europe, East Central Europe, Russia, East Asia, Latin America, or the Near and Middle East. The purpose of the area concentration is not to make an area specialist of the candidate, but rather to afford him a "laboratory sample" on which to focus his more general courses in international relations.[2] Whatever area the student selects, he must then complete eighteen semester hours of course work relating to that area. If the area chosen is Russia, for example, his area courses would be two in Russian history which together cover the period from the time of Peter the Great to the present, one course in Soviet economics, one on the political institutions of the Soviet Union, one on Soviet foreign policy, and one in Soviet literature.

During the first year of his two years of study, the candidate for the M.I.A. must take such courses in the language of the area on which he is concentrating as will enable him to read and write the language and use it orally. No student is permitted to register for the second year of the program who does not have reasonable facility in the language of the area of his concentration. Finally,

[1] *Announcement of the School of International Affairs 1956-1957*, Columbia University Bulletin of Information, Series 56, No. 31 (1956), p. 3.
[2] L. Gray Cowan, *A History of International Affairs and Associated Area Institutes, Columbia University* (New York: Columbia University Press, 1954), p. 30.

during the second year of the program, the student is required to prepare at least one major report in the field of his functional specialization—that is in the field of international economics in the case being discussed here. This is usually done in a seminar and is not as arduous an undertaking as a master's thesis. The report must satisfy the appropriate professor that the student has acquired competence in international economics. However, it is not expected that a candidate for the M.I.A. will master international economics to the extent required of a candidate for the doctorate in economics.

The pattern of the curricula for candidates for the M.I.A. who seek careers in international administration, international governmental relations, or in international business is much the same as that described for the student preparing in the field of international economics. That pattern is one of numerous courses specifically required and few electives spread over three categories —general courses in international relations, functional courses in a discipline, and courses about a specific geographic area.

Enrollment in the School of International Affairs is limited to persons preparing for nonacademic careers. Students at Columbia whose primary interest is teaching and research enroll as candidates for the Ph.D. in the Department of Public Law and Government (political science). In contrast to the rather rigidly prescribed curriculum for the M.I.A., the program leading to the Ph.D. in the Department of Public Law and Government, with emphasis on international law and relations, is one which permits considerable latitude. The student's two years of graduate course work (sixty semester hours) are planned in conjunction with an adviser to suit the student's individual needs. The courses for his primary field of interest, international law and relations, may be selected from a wide range of offerings including Basic Factors in World Politics, International Organization and Administration, International Law, Imperialism and International Relations, and courses dealing with the foreign policies of specific nations. The prospective candidate must also select a secondary field of interest which may be a combination of courses from any number of departments, selected with a view to the student's particular interests and needs. Usual minors are courses in foreign political institutions, political and social philosophy, or a program of studies selected from the offerings of one of Columbia's many geographic area institutions.

In addition to his course work, the candidate for the Ph.D. in public law and government must demonstrate the ability to use two foreign languages as research tools, he must pass a written examination on political theory, an oral examination on the subjects (not courses) of his primary and secondary fields of interest, and show accomplishment in research embodied in a dissertation.

FLETCHER SCHOOL OF LAW AND DIPLOMACY

Another and quite different approach to specialized training in international relations is illustrated by a description of the programs for the two-year master's degree and the Ph.D. offered by the Fletcher School of Law and Diplomacy at Tufts University. In contrast to the program for the M.I.A. at Columbia, which requires a student to develop both a functional and an area specialty, the Fletcher program emphasizes instruction in general international relations. The broad nature of the Fletcher program is evident in the kinds of careers for which it prepares students and in its admissions policy as well as in its curriculum.

The Fletcher program is designed to train students for careers in the Department of State and the diplomatic service of the United States, in the United Nations and other international agencies, in international business, finance, and journalism, as well as for careers in research and university teaching in international relations. Enrollment is limited to a maximum of fifty students entering in any one year. In addition to the usual requirements as to scholarship, Fletcher's admissions policy stresses breadth of undergraduate preparation, personal qualities, the nature of the applicant's interest in international affairs, and knowledge of a foreign language.

A broad liberal education is a prerequisite for admission because of the belief that "Education in international relations is in reality education for statesmanship, and perhaps no objective of education is less dependent upon the acquisition of a particular skill or of special information. No field of study is more dependent upon a broad knowledge and understanding of the accumulated thought and experience of mankind."[3] Since the Fletcher School does not teach the general subjects of the liberal arts, "its entire work depends upon and is conditioned by the prior study of history and the social sciences as well as languages."[4]

Personal qualifications for admission are assessed on the basis of four letters of recommendation. These letters must be submitted on a form prepared by the school, and the form is essentially a personality inventory. The personal qualifications of the applicant which each recommender is asked to appraise are as follows:

Character	Leadership ability
Honesty and integrity	Ability to work under pressure
Appearance and manner	Scholastic record of preparation
Common sense and judgment	Intellectual capacity
Emotional stability	Breadth of intellectual interests
General adaptability	Use of oral English
Cooperation	Use of written English
Initiative and independence	Public speaking
Promptness in completing	Definiteness of purpose
undertakings	General promise

As a part of the admissions process the applicant must submit a written statement giving the reasons for his choice of a career in the field of international affairs, along with a discussion of the plans for his life work. He must also possess a reading knowledge of one foreign language before he will be admitted. By means of the personality inventory and the applicant's written statement, officials at Fletcher attempt to determine before admitting an

---

[3] *Catalogue of the Fletcher School of Law and Diplomacy, 1956-57*, p. 13.
[4] *Loc. cit.*

applicant whether he has the personality traits desirable for a successful career in international relations. The effort made at Fletcher in this regard is one of the very few instances which can be cited where a graduate program gives formal attention to the personality factors required for the international relationist. The importance of giving that attention was discussed earlier, in chapter 2.

Nine fields of study are offered by the Fletcher School; these are grouped into three divisions. Division I covers the fields of international law (seven courses), international organization (five courses), and world politics (five courses). Division II embraces the fields of American diplomacy (five courses), European diplomacy (four courses), and special studies (ten courses in a variety of subjects such as Russian Diplomatic History, Postwar Asian Problems, Diplomatic Relations of the British Commonwealth of Nations, etc.). Division III consists of the fields of international trade and commercial policies (seven courses), international finance (five courses), and international economic relations (seven courses).

The normal study load is four courses per semester. Generally the requirements for the Master of Arts in Law and Diplomacy cannot be satisfied in less than four semesters, and the degree of doctor of philosophy in not less than six semesters. The candidate for the M.A.L.D. must pass an examination on four of the nine fields and all three divisions must be represented in his study program. The doctoral candidate is examined in six of the nine fields and all three divisions must also be represented in his program; however, he must select one of his six fields for concentrated study.

The M.A.L.D. program requires that the candidate have a reading knowledge of one modern foreign language, the Ph.D. program requires a thorough reading knowledge of two languages. A thesis is required for the former degree and a dissertation for the latter.

Classes at Fletcher are small and the seminar method is emphasized. Limited enrollment has enabled it to preserve an intimate atmosphere which is beneficial to an interchange of opinions and information between students and professors.

PRINCETON UNIVERSITY

The graduate program of the Woodrow Wilson School of Public and International Affairs at Princeton University represents still another approach to training specialists in international relations. Greater emphasis is placed on general training in the social sciences, particularly on the contributions of sociology, and less stress is given to courses specifically in international relations than at either Columbia or Fletcher.

The program at Princeton is designed to train students for careers "in business, in government, in labor, in journalism, or in international or military affairs." The educational philosophy of the school is that "Common to all of these pursuits is the factor of large-scale organization. The tensions between the individual and large-scale organizations, and between large-scale organizations themselves, are the critical tensions of our generation. Questions of war and peace, freedom and tyranny, prosperity and depression, cultural viability and social ennui hang upon these tensions and their resolution." Therefore, "Increasingly leadership in politics, government, business, and world affairs must come from those who have at their command the growing body of knowledge and analytical techniques and insights of the social science disciplines."[5] The departments of history, politics, and economics and sociology provide most of the teaching staff for the school, and numerous courses are taught by interdepartmental teams.

A number of teaching devices are utilized to approximate actual procedures in government and business. For example, the conference method and other forms of teamwork are employed to develop the student's capacity for cooperative work, and several

[5] *Graduate Program, Woodrow Wilson School of Public and International Affairs,* Official Register of Princeton University, XLVIII, No. 2 (1956), 8–9.

courses require that written material be presented in the form of brief reports to give students experience in writing concise memoranda, a skill that is much desired both in government and in business.

Admission is limited each year to twenty men. In all cases the applicant's personal qualities as well as his scholastic record are considered. A good grounding in the social sciences is desirable but not required if applicants show an exceptional record and promise.

A candidate for the degree of Master of Public Affairs normally takes twelve courses, three each during four semesters. Two two-semester courses are required: (1) American Institutions and Issues of Public Policy, and (2) Research and Policy-Making. The remaining eight semester courses are selected to meet the needs and interests of the individual student. These eight, in a typical program for one interested in a career in the Foreign Service, would be a two-semester course in Approaches and Methods in the Study of International Relations, a two-semester course in Problems in Political Economy, a one-semester course in Economic Growth and Social Change in Underdeveloped Areas, a one-semester course in Comparative Government, and finally, a one-semester course in Public Administration.

The course entitled Approaches and Methods in the Study of International Relations further illustrates the extensive interdisciplinary approach of the Woodrow Wilson School. The course is taught by an interdepartmental team, including a professor of sociology and the Bryant Professor of Geography and International Relations. It often includes in addition a representative from the Departments of Economics and/or History. The first semester of the course is devoted to a consideration of the uses and limitations in foreign policy analysis of the facts, concepts, hypotheses, and methods of the disciplines of geography, demography, political science, economics, and certain other systems of knowledge. The second semester is devoted to group study of selected policy problems. These differ from year to year.

One problem recently given students in this course was phrased as follows:

> During recent years a great deal has been said with regard to alleged interrelations between economic development, population increase, food supply, and political trends and behavior in the so-called underdeveloped countries. The United States government has extended some material and technical assistance to certain of these countries, for such stated purposes as raising living standards, combating communism, cementing political and military relationships with the United States, etc. The United States is also more or less committed to promoting simultaneously the growth and consolidation of democratic institutions in the countries aided.
>
> It has been widely asserted that these are incompatible objectives. In particular, it has been contended that attempts to increase economic production and to raise living standards in most underdeveloped countries is likely to result in explosive increase of population; and that, as Malthus predicted, population growth will tend to outrun food supply. It is predicted that rapid population increase, especially in the densely settled countries of Asia, will seriously disturb international relations and gravely threaten the security of the United States. It is argued that massive and very rapid industrialization, accompanied by active policies to curb population growth, alone can prevent this result; and that such developments, particularly rapid industrialization, probably cannot be carried out under democratic forms of government.
>
> As a special commission of experts, hypothetically appointed to advise the President, you are directed to investigate and appraise this cluster of issues, with respect to the underdeveloped countries in general, and with respect to India in particular; to formulate general principles that should govern United States action; and to prepare specific policy recommendations vis-à-vis India.

Students working for the degree of Master of Public Affairs with an emphasis in world relations are also required to acquire an effective reading knowledge of at least one foreign language. A summer internship is a further requirement. These are difficult to secure now that the Department of State has abandoned its internship program. However, interns have been placed in other agencies of the Federal Government, in departments of state and local government, as well as in business organizations. On occasion a student is permitted to substitute a summer abroad for the internship.

The required course in Research and Policy-Making referred to above usually features participation in research projects of interest to government or private agencies. For example, the project for 1955–56 concentrated on the issue of pressure-group attitudes toward the United Nations and was designed to fit into a study of public attitudes then being conducted by the Carnegie Endowment for International Peace. In each project a student group works under the direction of a faculty member or other experienced research director. Each student does a considerable amount of field work.

The program of the school is designed for persons wishing non-academic careers. The would-be international relationist who wishes to prepare for teaching enrolls in the Department of Politics (political science) to study for the Ph.D. This preparation normally requires full-time study for a period of two academic years. A candidate for the Ph.D. must qualify in six of eight fields: (1) political theory, (2) comparative political institutions, (3) American government, (4) constitutional law, (5) public administration, (6) public opinion and political parties, (7) international law and organization, and (8) international politics. In addition, the candidate must qualify in at least one cognate field (of the six required) outside of the Department of Politics. A student with a good undergraduate background in political science may take up to one-half of his Ph.D. program outside of the department, in such fields as sociology, psychology, history, economics, demography, etc. If he wishes to combine major work in political science with extensive specialization in a geographical area program, he may need more than two years to obtain the degree. However, with this kind of combined program, he normally is expected to offer only four of the eight fields in the Department of Politics.

YALE UNIVERSITY

The foregoing descriptions of programs at Columbia, Fletcher, and Princeton illustrate curricula organized within special schools of international relations or within departments of political science. There is a third type of organization for conducting graduate training—the interdepartmental committee. The program for the Ph.D. in international relations at Yale University is representative of the kind of training given under the auspices of an interdepartmental committee.

The committee at Yale is composed of representatives of the Departments of Economics, Geography, History, Political Science, and the Law School. "The program is designed to prepare students for teaching and research appointments in colleges and universities, for professional positions in government service, national and international, and for staff work with private, civic, and research organizations. The program also provides a social science background for foreign and international journalism."[6]

Satisfactory letters of recommendation and a report on the applicant's Graduate Record Examination scores are required for admission, as well as a high degree of distinction in his undergraduate scholastic record. An undergraduate major in political science or history, together with two or more courses in economics, is highly desirable, but a student whose major is in another field may be admitted provided his undergraduate work generally is of high quality. A student whose undergraduate training in the social sciences is deficient is expected to take more than the minimum number of courses required for the Ph.D. The minimum formal course work for the Ph.D. is two years, consisting of four courses per semester for four semesters.

The study program is divided into five fields, and students having no previous preparation in the five fields are required to take at least two graduate courses in each. The first field is international politics. In this field Yale provides such courses as Analysis of Policy and Power, Psychological and Cultural Factors in International Politics, Geography of World Power, and Strategic and Political Geography. The second field is methods and instruments

6 *Graduate School 1956–57,* Bulletin of Yale University, Series 52, No. 11 (1956), pp. 132–33.

of control, with offerings in International Organization and Administration, The United Nations System, and Contemporary International Law. The third field is the economics of international affairs, consisting of offerings in Economic Analysis and Its Applications, Foreign Central Banking and Monetary Systems, Foreign Monetary Policies and Experiences, Postwar International Monetary Policies, the Economy of Soviet Russia, Underdeveloped Areas and Economic Policy. Field four is comparative government and regional politics, which includes courses in Problems in the International Relations of Eastern Asia and the Pacific, Japanese Government and Politics, Soviet Foreign Policy, Comparative Government, Democracy and Dictatorship in Europe. The fifth field is American and European diplomatic history and foreign policies. In this field Yale gives such courses as European Diplomacy—1500 to the Present, European Diplomacy —1914–1939, and the History of American Foreign Policy and Diplomacy.

Candidates for the Ph.D. are required to demonstrate a reading knowledge of French and German, although on occasion Russian may be substituted for one of these. One language examination must be passed upon entrance to graduate study and the examination in the second not later than the beginning of the third semester of residence. A dissertation, of course, is one of the requirements.

Most students studying for the Ph.D. in this program take a master's degree as a matter of course. No thesis is required for the M.A., and it is awarded upon completion, with sufficient distinction, of a minimum of one year of course work covering four of the five fields named above. In lieu of the thesis the candidate is required to submit one or more seminar reports demonstrating analytical and interpretive skill. A reading knowledge of one language is also a requirement for the M.A.

The requirements for the Ph.D. in political science at Yale are similar to those for the Ph.D. in international relations, differing only in the fields of study. The prospective Ph.D. in political science selects three of six fields as the basis for his program: political theory, comparative government, public law, politics and policy formation, public administration, and finally, international politics and organization. He also takes one or two full-year courses outside the department of political science to profit by the contributions of other social sciences to the understanding of political phenomena.

Nation-wide, the curricula for doctor's degrees in political science with an emphasis on international relations are much the same as the programs at Princeton and Yale. Generally speaking, curricula for the Ph.D. in political science permit less course work specifically in world affairs and provide less opportunity for students to cross departmental lines than do the curricula for degrees in international relations *per se*.

The One-Year M.A.

Seven of the eight programs sketched above—two each at Columbia, Princeton, and Yale and one at Fletcher—are two-year programs. The seven additional programs outlined below are one-year curricula. It should be pointed out, however, that the designations "one" and "two" are somewhat theoretical. In practice, many candidates for a "two-year" M.A. or for a Ph.D. take five semesters to complete their course work and numerous candidates for a "one-year" degree complete their studies in not less than three semesters. The basic problem of any graduate curriculum in international relations, regardless of the length of time required for completion, is how to cover so vast a field of study. Needless to say, the difficulty is greater in a one-year course of study than in a two-year program.

University of Virginia

The Woodrow Wilson Department of Foreign Affairs has the responsibility for students working for the master's degree in foreign affairs at the University of Virginia. Twenty-four semester hours of course work are required for the M.A., but most candidates take not less than thirty-six hours of work in order to pass a final comprehensive examination which covers international politics, international law, international organization, international economics, American foreign policy, ideologies, and one geographic area.

There are three requirements for admission to study in the program at Virginia: (1) The applicant must possess a bachelor's degree with a grade average of at least B during his junior and senior years. (2) He must have had the equivalent of a two-semester course in international politics, preferably one semester in general international relations, and one semester of work on the foreign policies of the major nations. (3) He must have had another two-semester course in some field closely related to foreign affairs, such as European or American diplomatic history, international economics, or political geography.

There are no required courses in general international relations for the M.A. in foreign affairs. The candidate's subjects are selected largely to fill in the gaps in his undergraduate background of study as it is related to world affairs. His career objectives do not loom large in the selection of courses.

Standard courses in American foreign policy, international organization, international law, as well as problems seminars in these subjects are available. The department has developed a number of special offerings for international relations training including courses in Methods of Analysis and Theories of International Relations, Overseas Administration, Civil-Military Relations, Colonial Problems and International Relations, and Ideological Influences in International Relations.

Each M.A. candidate is required to select one year-long course (six semester hours) in a geographic area. A number of these are available: Latin America in World Affairs, The Near and Middle East in World Affairs, The Far East in World Affairs, Western Europe in World Affairs, Central Europe in World Affairs, etc. The purpose of the two-semester area course is to enable the student to see the basic elements of international relations at work in something smaller than the total world setting. There is no attempt to make an area expert out of the candidate, but rather to explain further the "cosmos" of general international relations by a concentration on the "microcosm" of one area.

A number of courses in the Virginia program give attention to skills required for the international relationist. The course in Foreign Policies of the United States, for example, attempts to develop capacity for teamwork. Students in the course are divided into teams to study major foreign policy decisions. In one instance, the question under discussion was whether the concessions made to the Soviet Union at the Yalta Conference were wise or unwise. One team of students evaluated the Yalta decisions in light of the knowledge generally available at the time of the decisions. Another team of two evaluated the decisions in light of the knowledge available at the time of this particular graduate project. Each team prepared a critique of the Yalta Conference. One member of each team presented the team's over-all evaluation to the class while the other member of each team defended his team's report in class discussion. During the year each member of the class served on three or four such teams.

In another seminar in the Virginia program, each student presents an oral report on a problem in international affairs, which is followed by class discussion. Each member of the seminar once during the year serves as a rapporteur for such a discussion. Thus, the seminar is utilized to give students experience in oral presentation and in reporting a meeting, as well as to obtain factual knowledge about the problem under discussion.

The Virginia program is typical of most M.A. programs in international relations in that a thesis is required for the degree. The topic must be one about which there is a considerable quantity of material available so that the student will have experience in investigating original sources such as government documents, diaries, and letters, and in learning how to collect, select, and order data around a clearly stated idea.

The Virginia program is atypical in that little emphasis is placed on foreign language. There is no language requirement for the M.A. if the applicant has earned twelve semester hours of undergraduate credit in a foreign language (twelve semester hours in one language or six semester hours in each of two languages, ancient or modern). Those who have not had this amount of undergraduate study of language may take a special examination to attest to a reading knowledge of a foreign language.

University of Denver

The one-year master's degree program at the University of Denver is similar to the one at the University of Virginia in that it is planned to build on the student's undergraduate background. However, the selection of graduate courses for which a degree candidate enrolls is based on a somewhat different formula from that used at Virginia.

Course work consists of the satisfactory completion of a minimum of forty-five quarter hours (thirty semester hours) of graduate offerings. One year-long course (seven and one-half quarter hours; that is, five semester hours) given by the Department of International Relations is required. The remaining hours are elective, and all may be taken in other departments.

The candidate's undergraduate and graduate courses, considered as a single group, must show study in five fields *insofar as they relate to international affairs:* (1) modern history, (2) political science, (3) economics, (4) geography, and (5) human relations (sociology, psychology, and anthropology). A qualifying examination, administered by the Department of International Relations, determines the adequacy of the candidate's undergraduate background in each field. He is then enrolled in graduate courses in those fields in which he shows weaknesses.

The graduate course required of all candidates for the M.A. is The Core and Scope of International Relations. It is designed as an integrator. A conceptual framework is developed to enable the student to understand how his multidisciplinary studies fit together as applied to international problems. The course also gives considerable attention to sources and techniques for research in the field of international relations.

All five professors in the Department of International Relations are present for all class meetings of Core and Scope. Two or three of the staff participate in the International Relations Seminar. Other departmental courses are conducted by a single teacher. A thesis and a reading knowledge of one foreign language are additional requirements for the Master of Arts in International Relations.

The student's program is not tailored with a specific career in mind on the assumption that at the master's level "a broad understanding of the many forces which shape international society and affect the relations between states . . . provides the best basis for success in relevant careers in government service, international organizations, teaching, adult education and research."[7]

THE "NO-THESIS" OPTION

Still another type of master's degree program is the one which permits the student to substitute additional course work in lieu of a thesis, if he so chooses. The program at the University of Connecticut is a case in point. Students who write a thesis are required to take a minimum of fifteen semester hours of graduate work, whereas those who elect to substitute additional course work must earn not less than twenty-four graduate credits. The experience of the University of Connecticut that virtually all degree candidates elect not to write a thesis is typical of the recent experience in institutions which offer this option.

The list of courses which the University of Connecticut Department of Government and International Relations will approve for the master's degree is flexible, geared to the needs of the candidate; no specific courses are required. However, anyone going

[7] *The Master's Degree Program in International Relations at the University of Denver* (Mimeographed; Denver: Social Science Foundation, 1956), p. 1.

through the program is almost certain to take the Seminar in International Relations and the Seminar in American Diplomacy. It is most likely that he will also take Advanced Comparative Government and European Diplomacy Since 1814. He may possibly take the offering in Research Methods in Government. All these courses are offered by the Department of Government and International Relations. Beyond these courses, the student usually rounds out his program by taking courses offered in other departments.

Work in international economics, given by the Department of Economics, is strongly recommended by advisers, but as in all institutions where such study is not specifically required there is frequently a high degree of student resistance to including economics in the program. A course frequently recommended to students is one in Political Psychology, offered by the Department of Psychology. This course includes such topics as personality characteristics of the politician, the political stereotype, formation of political attitudes, the role of public opinion and propaganda in politics, and national character studies.

The program at Connecticut deviates from the nation-wide pattern in that it does not provide a graduate course in international organization. It is expected, however, that a candidate for the M.A. will have had undergraduate study in this field; if he has not, then ordinarily he is expected to fill in this gap by taking the university's undergraduate course in International Organization without receiving graduate credit for it. The program is also not typical of the majority of curricula in the United States in that there is no foreign language requirement for the M.A. degree.

The entrance requirements at Connecticut are representative of those at many other institutions. Admission is defined in three requirements: (1) having a bachelor's degree with an undergraduate grade average of C+, (2) having an average mark of B or better in the last two years of undergraduate work, or at least an average of B in the major field, (3) ordinarily having an undergraduate major in political science.

M.A. IN POLITICAL SCIENCE WITH EMPHASIS
ON INTERNATIONAL RELATIONS

The programs at the Universities of Virginia, Denver, and Connecticut are illustrative of one-year curricula organized within a special department of international relations. Students in those programs work for the M.A. in international relations *per se.* More typical of general practice in institutions of higher education is the organization of the study program within the department of political science with the candidate for a degree working for the M.A. in political science with emphasis on international relations. Under this latter arrangement, generally speaking, students are permitted less interdisciplinary work than in the case of those who work for degrees in international relations *per se.* However, depending upon the institution, a student's program is not completely confined to the department of political science. Descriptions of several programs will illustrate this generalization.

At the University of Wisconsin, for example, fourteen of the minimum of eighteen semester hours of course work required for the master's degree in political science must be obtained in the department. The department offers some thirty courses in international law, international affairs, international organization, American foreign policy, and governments of foreign countries for the student choosing to specialize in international relations. A knowledge of American government is also expected, and a thesis is required. Before he is admitted to work for the M.A. the candidate is normally expected to have had the equivalent of an undergraduate major in political science (thirty semester hours) and a minimum of twenty-four semester hours' work in one foreign language.

The work for the master's degree in political science at the University of Florida consists of thirty semester hours of registration including twenty-four hours of course work plus six hours in research and thesis. Twelve of the twenty-four hours of course work must be concentrated within two of seven fields: (1) political theory, (2) American government and politics, (3) comparative government, (4) international relations and organizations, (5) international law and organization, (6) public law, (7) public administration. In addition, a minor of six semester hours must be completed in a separate but related discipline, usually geography or history or economics. Knowledge of one foreign language is required.

Specialization in international relations with political science as the home department at the University of Oregon is also representative of the situation in a number of institutions.

The University of Oregon offers a number of approaches to students who wish to concentrate their graduate training in international relations, although the degrees granted must be in one of the existing departments since no departmental or interdepartmental degree is available in international relations *per se*.

The most direct recognition of international relations as an area for graduate concentration is made by the Department of Political Science. That department offers a special program leading to the master's degree in political science, but provides sufficient flexibility to permit outside courses pertinent to international relations to be counted as a part of the major program. Presumably the decision as to what is and what is not pertinent to the program and how much work will be accepted from other departments is up to the advisor. This program makes it possible for the student to include in his major work all the upper division courses and seminars devoted directly and chiefly to international relations regardless of departments. It should also be noted again that this leads to the M.A. in Political Science although the concentration may be actually directed toward the general area of international relations.

. . . .

The offering of the University of Oregon in the field of international relations is rather extensive and distributed among various departments of the College of Liberal Arts so that the coverage is broad in both approach and content. In the Departments of History, Political Science, Economics, Geography, and Anthropology there are faculty members whose interests are more or less closely tied with international aspects of their disciplines. For the student interested in directing his university training along these lines there appear adequate opportunities. . . .

. . . .

The subcommittee wishes to call attention to the fact that much time and thought were devoted to the advisability of recommending the establishment of a degree in international relations at this time. This was unanimously rejected on the grounds that: (1) present degree offerings permit the same concentration as would be included in such degrees, and (2) because international relations as a field is not yet sufficiently well-defined to warrant its carrying the degree designation.[8]

M.A. in Citizenship and World Affairs
at Western Reserve University

Another curriculum, a unique one, is the program leading to the master's degree in citizenship and world affairs at Western Reserve University. Although the program is presently dormant for lack of financial support, it merits description as an example of what can be done by combining academic training in world affairs with training in certain specific skills.

The program was designed to provide a sound background of international relations study along with a practical proficiency in the organization and administration of community education. Graduates of this program today occupy significant positions with World Affairs Councils, in the Division of Public Services of the Department of State, and in a variety of private organizations concerned with foreign affairs.

Admission was limited to graduates from accredited colleges with a major in one of the social sciences who had shown evidence of distinguished leadership in college extracurricular activities. The curriculum consisted of thirty-six semester hours of work. Thirty of these were taken in courses similar to those offered in most M.A. programs in international relations; that is, selected to fill in the gaps in the student's undergraduate background in international politics, international organization, international economics, diplomatic history, geography, and the behavioral sciences. The remaining six semester hours were in the form of a seminar and on-the-job training given by the Cleveland Council on World Affairs. This particular seminar required

---

[8] "The Role of the University of Oregon in World Affairs," *Universities and World Affairs,* Document No. 61 (Mimeographed; New York: Carnegie Endowment for International Peace, 1954), pp. 16–17.

twelve clock hours of work at the council each week for nine months. Students worked under supervision within every department of the council to get an understanding of the operation of each department. Work included maintaining membership files, promoting and publicizing council activities, assisting with fund-raising and membership drives. Students were also given specific responsibilities in connection with the council's discussion groups, its radio and television programs, and its materials-distribution program. Later in the year each degree candidate was made responsible for the planning, development, and execution of an individual education project. As an example of this kind of project, one student developed a program for the study of the United Nations Charter for a high school group.

Along with this on-the-job activity conducted by the council, the students participated in a seminar concerned with the analysis of resources available in a community for the study of world affairs, the organization and financing of a World Affairs Council, the function and use of committees and of volunteers in community education work. The seminar also dealt with techniques for leading group discussions and the uses to be made of pamphlets, maps, charts, and audio-visual aids. The theory and philosophy of work in community education in world affairs were considered at length; on-the-job activities tested the theory and philosophy in actual operation.

Summary

The nature of specialized training programs in international relations was described in chapters 1 and 2. To facilitate presentation of the general picture of such training throughout American colleges and universities very few examples were given and references to specific programs were kept to a minimum. Comments in the first two chapters largely were confined to generalizations based on the many sources consulted in the preparation of this report. The generalizations have been illustrated in chapter 3 by outlining fifteen graduate programs in eleven institutions.

The fifteen sketches show something of the diversity of training programs. For example, the School of International Affairs at Columbia University stresses the development of a functional specialization and an understanding of one geographic area in connection with instruction in general international relations, whereas the Fletcher School at Tufts and the Woodrow Wilson School at Princeton emphasize broad generalized training. The generalized program at Fletcher focuses on the political, diplomatic, and economic aspects of international relations whereas the Princeton program is even broader, encompassing more of the social sciences. Programs within departments of political science such as the one at Wisconsin tend to be somewhat less multidisciplinary than programs conducted under the auspices of an interdepartmental committee (Yale) or those organized in a special department of international relations (Denver).

In the main, programs for the graduate study of international relations are eclectic; that is, the course of study for any student is formulated in light of his undergraduate background and is built with a view to his career objectives. The curriculum of Columbia's School of International Affairs with its rather rigidly prescribed series of courses is representative of only a few programs in the United States. The free choice of courses given students in most programs means that it is possible for two students graduated from the same institution and each trained in international relations to have gone through a quite different series of courses. However, the free choice allowed in most curricula has not led to such a chaotic situation in fact as it appears in theory that it might.

Although few institutions have specifically required courses, most students in most programs are urged to enroll in and do take a basic core of courses in general international relations which includes study of international politics, international organization, and European diplomatic history. In addition, most students in most institutions take some work in the fields of international law and international economics. It is after students have taken the basic core of courses common to most curricula that study programs tend to become highly individualized.

The sketches in this chapter have illustrated other characteristics of specialized training in international relations. They have shown the efforts made to integrate this multidisciplinary field of study by means of the area course (Virginia), the single integrative course (Denver), the course which is cooperatively taught, and the problems course (Princeton). The programs outlined have shown that insofar as skills are concerned, the principal concern of "producers" of international relations specialists is with research and analysis. But the program at Western Reserve University, for example, demonstrates the possibility of building programs in international relations which can develop skills other than research and analysis. The sketches show that few programs give attention to the personality traits desirable for the specialist; the admissions policy of Fletcher is illustrative of at least one action which can be taken in this regard. The reactions of students who have been trained in these and other programs are reported in the next chapter.

CHAPTER 4

Strengths and Weaknesses of Specialized Training as Seen by Former Students

THE OBSERVATIONS in the preceding chapters about specialized training in international relations have been based on the views of "producers," "consumers," and "products," that is, professors who train specialists in international relations, employers of such specialists, and former graduate students in international relations who are now employed as specialists. This chapter is devoted exclusively to the opinions of the "products."

One hundred fifty-two holders of graduate degrees in international relations (or degrees in political science with emphasis on international relations) were queried during the preparation of this report. The 152 persons were selected as follows: the person heading the graduate training program in each of fifty-one universities which have extensive instructional programs designed to train specialists in international relations was asked to supply the names and addresses of four or five of the institution's graduates, now known to be holding positions as international relations specialists. Time, and the expense involved, permitted personal interviews with only a small number of the persons whose names were supplied; questionnaires were sent to the others. The questionnaire allowed ample space for free replies, and many of those returned were accompanied by letters elaborating on the replies contained in the questionnaire itself. To facilitate frank replies, all respondents were assured that their comments would be regarded as confidential, and that neither their names nor the

names of their graduate schools would be used in reporting results. Of the 152 respondents, ninety-five had received the M.A.
only, and fifty-seven had received the Ph.D. as well as the M.A.
The degrees were granted between 1923 and 1954, with the majority in the period 1941–52.

The persons surveyed were requested to evaluate certain specific aspects of their training. Some generalizations based on these
responses have been reported in earlier chapters. In addition,
those surveyed were asked to comment on what they believed
were the principal strengths and weaknesses of their training in
light of the kind of work in which they were engaged. It is these
evaluations of strengths and weaknesses which are reported in this
chapter. Evaluations differed, depending on the position held by
the respondent, the character of the curriculum under which he
studied, and on the nature of his undergraduate preparation.
However, replies were not as varied as one might expect. The
comments from some 50 respondents quoted below are for the
most part typical of the opinions expressed by many of the 152
persons. All persons quoted in this chapter hold a degree in international relations *per se* unless otherwise specified. When the
master's degree is mentioned it refers to the one-year M.A. unless
qualified by the designation "two-year." The evaluations are divided into three groups representing replies received from persons employed by the Federal Government, those holding positions as teachers, and, finally, respondents engaged in other kinds
of work.

Employees of the Federal Government

Respondent Number 1 is a Foreign Service officer who looked
forward to a career in the Foreign Service from the time he enrolled in college as a freshman. He took an undergraduate major
in government and a minor in economics. His master's degree was
in political science with emphasis on international relations, and
his doctoral studies were of the same combination. He feels that

his graduate training in the main was useful preparation for a dozen different posts he has held in the Service. Its chief weakness

was its failure to prepare me for a life spent in great part outside the United States. I refer here to practical problems—language, geography, international trade, and to a more general lacuna in the field of European and Asian diplomatic and military history. Also, at the time I did my graduate training 20 years ago the courses in International Politics, Law, and Organization were too diffuse and topical. Because of the emphasis on current topics most of the information is completely obsolete. Learning to present materials orally is particularly important to my present work. I had to learn the hard way. Formal training would have been of great help. I had no courses in geography which was also a great mistake.

Respondent Number 2 is also a Foreign Service officer. His principal duties are political reporting and some negotiation. He acquired an undergraduate major in political science and a minor in history. His M.A. was in political science with an emphasis on international relations, and his Ph.D. in international relations *per se.*

The language requirements for my graduate work were helpful, but before I entered the Foreign Service I could not speak a language. Nevertheless the background was a foundation on which I could build a speaking knowledge. I had no economics in graduate school, but my undergraduate courses were good and in these days when the political has become the politico-economic it is most important that this field be covered. I never had a course in geography after leaving high school. This was a mistake although I was able to make it up by self-study. The ability to express oneself orally is an important item and should be covered more adequately. I had public speaking in high school and did some debating in college but that was not enough.

Respondent Number 3, a Foreign Service officer serving as a vice-consul, has an undergraduate major in political science with a minor in history, an M.A. in political science with an emphasis on comparative government, and a Ph.D. in political science with an emphasis on international relations. The emphasis on international relations consisted of study in the fields of comparative government and the history of particular geographic areas rather than courses in generalized international relations.

I consider my graduate training to have been generally ineffective. This is said with full knowledge of the tendency to overvalue recent practical experience and to underestimate the stimulation and direction at the time of the graduate instruction. Why do I consider it generally ineffective? (1) Because there was no unity in knowledge, no beginning, no motives, no movement. There was only the docile submission to courses selected at random without either the courses or the instructors capable of integrating the material at hand. (2) Because the professors were almost always concerned primarily with doing their research. They usually taught from old notes while exhausting themselves on the scholarly writing necessary to maintain their personal status among their colleagues. They could never conceal their boredom with the necessity of teaching or counseling students. (3) Because the professors lacked courage. The human weakness—jealousy, rivalry, fear of taking an unpopular position—too often made the professors less than respected intellectual leaders. (4) They usually managed to remove the most important factor in international relations of this or any era—namely, *man* and his nature.

But there were exceptions to each of these criticisms in the form of professors whom I distinctly remember and who stimulated and drove me to learn. Incidentally, in no case was any close personal acquaintanceship established. These men moved and guided me with the power of their thought and their manner of presentation. They perhaps represent the difference between my being somewhat educated (or at least interested) in foreign relations, and being only academically oriented in foreign questions.

Respondent Number 4 has an undergraduate major in international relations with a minor in American history, and a master's degree in political science with an emphasis on international relations. He is critical of his study for the M.A. in terms of his position as a vice-consul.

The required courses in Constitutional Law and Public Opinion may be generally useful but are not necessarily relevant to a person working in the Foreign Service. The chief strength of my graduate training was learning how to go about finding information, sorting, assembling, interpreting, and finally presenting it, rather than in the actual knowledge obtained.

Respondent Number 5 is a Foreign Service officer whose principal duties are those of a consul. His undergraduate major is history with a minor in economics. He earned a master's degree in international relations, a second master's degree in political science, and a Ph.D. in political science with an emphasis on international relations. The institution from which he obtained the doctorate permitted a great deal of work outside the department of political science.

The interdisciplinary seminars, in which historians, economists and sociologists participated, were of especial value. My graduate training gave me the intellectual courage to support unpopular doctrine with rational argument and showed me the importance of so doing. In a time of conformity this could perhaps be called a weakness; I prefer to consider it a strength. If my graduate training lacked anything it was experience in how to write *briefly*. I also believe that International Law and Organization are generally overemphasized academically. I have found little use in my present work for study in these fields.

Respondent Number 6, another Foreign Service officer, has an undergraduate major in history, a minor in modern language, and a master's degree in international relations. He feels that the strength of his M.A. is that it

gave me a broad, integrated picture of the world at the end of World War II and gave me an appreciation of the political, economic, legal, and cultural interdependency of nations and people. I gained a perspective of the role which the U. S. will play in that world for the next century.

The principal weakness of his training was

its brevity. I should have liked an additional year and I resented some of the pedagogic methods which made me waste time studying for monthly, quarterly tests and examinations. I knew what I wanted to learn and did not waste time. I often felt that I was obliged to study to pass the professor's course instead of preparing myself for my chosen career. I think graduate schools place too little emphasis on personality factors in admitting students into the field of international relations. The creeps and bookworms have little to contribute to the practical aspects of our field. I would have been much better off if I had taken more work in international economics and concentrated less on international law.

Respondent Number 7, a vice-consul, has an undergraduate major in international relations and a minor in economics, as well as a master's degree in international relations. He indicates that his generalized training is extremely useful in his work. "The principal weakness was the failure to learn how to prepare good, clear, brief written statements."

Respondent Number 8 is an administrative officer in a government agency engaged in intelligence work. He has an undergraduate major in international relations, as well as two M.A.'s in international relations from different universities. He reports satisfaction with his generalized training except for the fact that occasionally it was

too bookish. The majority of my duties, I have found, entail dealing with people as well as with ideas and/or procedures. Therefore I feel strongly on the need for more sociology, psychology, management, writing and oral presentation study, either in graduate or undergraduate work. No matter how great the idea, the implementation of it requires dealing with or through other people. Your success depends therefore on how well you can obtain cooperation of others in the implementation of your plans. This I cannot emphasize too strongly. You must work *with* other human beings and your success in your job depends primarily on how well you can work with others.

Respondent Number 9 is an officer in the Department of State. During the course of his formal education he obtained an undergraduate major in economics and three graduate degrees: two M.A.'s and a Ph.D., all in international relations.

My graduate training covered adequately the fields that I have found it necessary to use in my job; I would hesitate to prescribe any material improvement in it. However, I am inclined to believe that too much emphasis is placed on meticulous, painstaking research for a dissertation. The time could be better spent in essay-type projects and in broader-gauge study. There ought to be more philosophy and search for general understanding and less pedantry.

Respondent Number 10, with an undergraduate major in political science and a minor in French, and a master's degree in international relations, is supervising area research in a government organization. He feels that the generalized approach of his graduate instruction, covering diplomatic history, law, and economics has been invaluable to him, and the principal weakness of his instruction was the absence of any emphasis on sociological and psychological factors in international affairs. Like most of the respondents who are engaged in research making use of foreign languages, he found that there had been insufficient emphasis on a foreign language requirement in his graduate program. He adds, also,

It has been my experience as an administrator that the *greatest* deficiency of the American graduate student is his inability to write clearly, concisely, and quickly.

Respondent Number 11 is employed as a political intelligence analyst with the Department of State. He has an undergraduate major in history with a minor in English, and an M.A. in international relations.

Although my general work in international politics never has been really translatable to job requirements, I feel that such training has been invaluable. From the perspective of my present position, lack of training in comparative economic systems and international trade I feel was the principal weakness of my graduate training. I would also strongly recommend that any international relations graduate student take courses in political or economic geography. The single greatest asset of my graduate instruction was the rigorous training I received in research.

Respondent Number 12 is employed by a government agency as an intelligence research specialist on the Soviet area. He has an undergraduate major in political science with a minor in history, a master's degree in international relations, and a Ph.D. in political science with an emphasis on the U.S.S.R.

Peculiar as it may sound, I was never required to take any courses in economics. This has been a major weakness in my training. Neither did I have any systematic work in geography. What little I know was picked up from history, political science and general international relations courses. A one-semester course in geography should be a must for anyone going into my type of work. Very little attention was given to my written work; the only criticisms I received were marginal comments. I feel that this lack of assistance in organization and analysis of written work has been a detriment to me in my present position. Certainly the chief strength of my training for my present job was my study of the Soviet area.

Respondent Number 13, with an undergraduate major in international relations and a master's degree in the same field, is serving as a military intelligence research specialist. He reports complete satisfaction with his generalized training in international relations for his current job. However,

> I feel particularly deficient in foreign languages. Among my friends and co-workers the inability to command effectively one or more foreign languages is probably one of the principal obstacles to their advancement in the field of research. The effectiveness of the training I received I would ascribe in large measure to the free discussion and debate between students, both in and out of class, particularly when there were a number of foreign students participating. The informal social contacts between students and members of the faculty which my graduate department encouraged were certainly the highlight of my training.

Respondent Number 14 is a research analyst for the Department of State engaged in research on the Soviet area. His undergraduate major is in international relations, and his M.A. in the same field. He earned the Ph.D. in political science and took an additional year of study in a Russian area program. He feels that the area competence which he added to his generalized training has been of the most use to him in his present work. The principal criticism of his graduate training is the

> excessive time spent in seminars, on reports requiring lengthy research in minutiae. This could better have been spent doing extensive reading to fill in the gaps remaining after undergraduate courses.

Respondent Number 15 has an undergraduate major in economics. The institution where he studied for the M.A. in international relations required no thesis, but the curriculum placed a great deal of emphasis on group discussion and brief written reports. He is serving as a liaison officer with an American Embassy overseas. His criticism of his general work in international relations is

> the lack of training in arriving at practical solutions to given problems in the fields of politics and economics. Too many problems were presented and not enough attempt was made to arrive at solutions.

Respondent Number 16 is in charge of administering a technical assistance program abroad. He has an undergraduate major in international relations, and his Ph.D. is in the same field. His doctoral work was done under an interdepartmental committee.

The chief strength of my graduate training was the fact that I escaped from the rigid pattern of course work within a single department and was permitted to branch off on my own into sociology, social psychology, economics and statistics. However, the work was poorly coordinated and there was no attempt to relate the various fields of social science.

Respondent Number 17 took an undergraduate major in history and a minor in political science; his M.A. and Ph.D. are in international relations. He is serving as a public affairs officer with the United States Information Agency. He has no criticism of his two graduate degrees in international relations as preparation for his present position except for the lack of more than one course in international economics.

Twelve of the persons with whom the writer corresponded are members of the Armed Forces serving in a variety of positions as instructors in some type of military organization, or as military attachés with embassies, or as liaison officers with other governmental agencies. The comments of military personnel on their graduate instruction, which in nearly every case is a master's degree in international relations, are much the same as the comments from other government employees. The exceeding importance of personality factors is stressed. For example, one man, holding the rank of major, emphasizes that

Personality factors assume an importance out of proportion to skill and knowledge, especially when a consolidated "Army" position on a political issue is desired. Trying to get professional civilian academicians, political appointees and professional soldiers to agree is *difficult*.

Another officer writes in the same vein:

I attended graduate school as a Regular Army officer knowing that I had to be, by Army regulations, put into a job utilizing the education I received at government expense. I received this type of assignment but found that my political training left me in a rather peculiar position. My superiors and contemporaries in the Army who had not had this type of outside civilian training thought I was a rather confused, permeable politician whose mind no longer comprehended military realities. My compatriots in other departments of government, with whom I had to coordinate and collaborate daily, thought I had a stupid, backward, inflexible military type of mind. I am not sure whether my position was complimentary or not but it was interesting and challenging.

I think Defense did well to send some of us "militarists" to school to learn international politics. I believe the interdependence of military realities and political maneuverings today are such that the Department of State would do well to send more of its people to our high-level military schools.

Another comment found occasionally on the replies from military personnel, as well as from other persons employed by the Federal Government, is the lack of practicality of the college training. One Army officer writes:

Practical examples were not stressed enough. There is too great a tendency on the part of instructors to teach theory and not tie it up with the everyday problems we face.

All the evaluations reported above came from persons with specialized training in international relations. In the course of seeking the reaction of specialists to their graduate instruction, the writer talked with and corresponded with many persons employed in the field of international relations who are subject-matter experts according to the definitions adopted for use in this volume. The comments of some of these experts are of interest in evaluating the training of the international relationist. One reply came from an economist working in the International Monetary Fund, and another from an economist with the International Bank for Reconstruction and Development. Each has an undergraduate major in economics and graduate degrees emphasizing international economics. Neither feels his work requires instruction in general international relations. However, another respondent employed by the Department of State as an international economist has two graduate degrees from an institution which emphasizes general international relations as a part of training in international economics.

The chief strength of my training was a broad and well-balanced program covering history, law and economics and not restricted to one geographic area.

Another respondent with an undergraduate major in economics as well as an M.A. and a Ph.D. in that field is also an international economist in the Department of State. He feels the lack of a broader background and indicates that in his present position it would be desirable to have more training in international politics, political theory, international organization, and the behavioral sciences. In addition, he points out that

research techniques of people coming into the Department of State are not well developed, but this can be fairly quickly remedied on the job. Inadequate writing skills are a more serious matter. Almost everyone engaged in research in the government could stand improvement. In the Department of State there is probably no one thing that is more lacking in people coming in new than an ability to write well. They all develop a certain skill as time goes on but much of it is still bad. Personally, I had no training during graduate work. I often feel the lack even though I have not run into any serious trouble. The small measure of success in writing seems to be more the result of the nature of writing about economic matters than of any high skill on my part. Inadequacy in writing is more glaring among those who write about political as opposed to economic matters.

Another reply was received from a veterinarian who is acting as the adviser to the government in an underdeveloped area on livestock disease of economic importance and animal diseases of public health importance. He has had no work whatsoever in the field of international relations. All of his graduate study was strictly technical. The respondent emphasizes that it was necessary for him to make use of anthropological, economic, and political studies pertaining to the various countries in which he has worked, as well as to acquire language training. He adds:

If personality factors do not match the technical qualifications, a person doesn't last very long in this work. Patience and perseverance are the qualities most required.

Another respondent is a forestry expert with an undergraduate major as well as a master's and doctor's degree in that field. He is working overseas and complains of the

overemphasis on technical training in all my education, and not enough guidance in successful human relations. Successful human relations are fully 90 percent of my position. Perhaps one should not expect this from graduate study but it is certainly significant how some instructors being broad in their outlook are helpful in this regard, and others are narrowly confined to their subjects.

Still another questionnaire was received from a professional engineer, serving the United States Government overseas. He replied with some feeling.

My answers to you are based on personal experience and contacts with diplomats, U.N. employees, sales representatives, financial experts, economists, and engineers. I have realized my own shortcomings and my countrymen have revealed theirs to me on many occasions. When I see a man blundering along, I am guilty of prying into his academic background. It happens that our State Department is quite often held in low regard abroad because of the shortcomings of the individuals and their ignorant handling of what appear to be very simple items. This is usually traced back to the lack of proper education. I have never taken university subjects in foreign affairs and am therefore not qualified to judge the professors in that field. However, I am qualified to judge the products. . . .

Yesterday I had lunch with five friends from the United States—an investment advisor with fifteen years' overseas service, an advertiser with fourteen years' overseas experience, a vice-president of one of the largest United States corporations with over twenty years overseas, and two other engineers. Their general recommendations are as follows: (1) a professional or business administration degree for diplomatic and also commercial overseas personnel; (2) one year with a U.S. firm in the States practicing his degree or his business specialty before going overseas, either with the State Department or a firm, to gain perspective of business or professional practices in the United States; (3) special training for the foreign work. In the special training the most important subject should be physical and economic geography to orient the individual on the physical factors which determine climate, resources, industry, and the factors which give each foreign country its individual character. The next subject would be business law and contracts, to give him a base for comparison. Third would be hygiene, health, and sanitation for his own protection. Fourth would be language of the country in which he would be working, and it was agreed that the candidate should pass a practical conversational examination before he left the U.S.A.

Another reply came from the first secretary of a United States Embassy, who has not gone through a formal training program in international relations although he has taken two or three in-

dividual courses. His undergraduate major is in business administration, his minor in geology. His master's degree is in economics,
and his Ph.D. in agricultural economics.

> In looking back I do not regret at all having dabbled in various fields
> of study, and in fact I believe it would have been helpful to have ob-
> tained an even broader background. For this reason I recommend that
> those who plan to work in the field of international affairs would do
> better if they obtained to the maximum extent a background in as
> many fields as possible, rather than specializing in intensive study of
> foreign politics, history, or geography. I have been very strongly im-
> pressed with the fact that it is relatively easy to obtain the detail during
> on-the-job training but that it is very difficult to obtain the over-all,
> general background which should be the goal of general liberal arts
> training.

It is clear that graduates of international relations curricula
who now hold positions in the Federal Government evaluate international relations training in much the same way as do their
employees whose opinions have been reported in chapter 2. There
is considerable agreement among the specialists and their employers that the chief strength of training programs is the broad
view of foreign policy problems which curricula give students.
The principal weaknesses of most training programs are: inadequate instruction in economics, geography, and the behavioral
sciences, the failure to develop the skill of writing clearly and
concisely, and weakness in screening prospective specialists to exclude those who lack those personality traits necessary for successful service in government.

Teachers

The completed questionnaires received from persons with specialized training in international relations and who are now engaged in teaching tend to divide into two groups. Those professors with heavy teaching loads and little time for research criticize
the language requirements for their graduate degrees as having
been useless. They also feel that the writing of a doctoral dissertation has contributed little to their effectiveness as teachers. The

other group, those who devote more time to research, also tend to be critical of the language requirement. The criticism, however, is that insufficient language skill was required. Those in this second group believe that the experience of writing a dissertation has been a valuable one. Also, teachers frequently express the belief that graduate study did not permit sufficient time for reflection on, and discussion of, reading assignments and research projects.

Respondent Number 1 in the group of teachers has an undergraduate major in history and a minor in political science. She received no master's degree, but took her doctorate in international relations under an interdepartmental committee arrangement. She is teaching one course in American government, a general introduction to political science, and one introductory course in international relations.

Because of the interdepartmental nature of my graduate study, I became aware of the interrelatedness of knowledge and gained some introductory insight into fields outside of political science. However, effective teaching requires some knowledge of, and ability to use, teaching tools as well as knowledge of the subject matter. I feel, therefore, limited work at the graduate level in education courses would be helpful to gain some knowledge of teaching methods, particularly if no undergraduate work in such courses has been taken. A limited course in teaching methods might have saved some agony for my students as I learned and am learning teaching on the job.

The undergraduate major of respondent Number 2 is in political science with a minor in history. His M.A. and Ph.D. were taken in political science with an emphasis on international relations. The additional fact that he had served with the Corps of Engineers during World War II appealed to one college department head who sought someone who could "talk in engineering terms and sell the value of social science" to students in a technical school. The respondent teaches courses in introduction to social science, American government, constitutional law, and international politics. His graduate program permitted considerable crossing of departmental lines, which he feels is of great value to him in his present job. However, no opportunity was given in his graduate work for the oral presentation of materials.

I believe that a well-organized departmental program orienting its people to teaching might be devised so that the student could present lectures, talks, discussions in his own field before students interested in the same subject, and thus perfect his abilities to disseminate material to others.

Respondent Number 3 was preparing for teaching when he took his undergraduate major in political science, and his master's and doctor's degrees in political science with an emphasis on international relations. He was a teaching assistant during four years of graduate study and regarded this experience as

one of the great strengths in my graduate training. It brought me into closer contact with faculty for the development of skill in the discipline and gave me invaluable experience in teaching and administration, as well as providing contacts with men of some experience in the profession outside of the university. We had special meetings of teaching assistants in which various aspects of the teacher's life at large and small institutions, as well as other types of employment open to students in my discipline, were considered. We frequently discussed the problems which teachers face. This was invaluable preparation for teaching.

Respondent Number 3 has an especial interest in psychology and took courses in that subject as part of his graduate program.

I found them of no particular use, since they were oriented for specialists in psychology and were not adapted for use by the student of international relations.

Respondent Number 4 received his Ph.D. in political science with an emphasis on international relations. He took his degree in 1941 and now devotes his time almost exclusively to graduate teaching and supervision of graduate instruction in international relations in a large department of international relations. In view of his present work, he feels a great weakness in his graduate training was the lack of instruction in economics even though he has an undergraduate major in that field.

I had about as fine a program of studies and experience at the graduate level as could be obtained at that time. It would, however, be considered quite inadequate now. Teaching international relations involves a broader basis of approach than one might acquire through the formal process of graduate instruction in political science and one related field. A principal asset of my training was experience as a teaching assistant, which provided an excellent opportunity for contact with fine professors. The greatest distinction between reading a list of books and a sound program of graduate instruction comes from the personal contact with the instructor. Here the personality factor, the ability of the instructor to impart to the student some perception and feeling of the subject, a frame of reference, and the lessons of personal observations and experience are all-important.

Respondent Number 5 has an undergraduate degree in education, and his M.A. and Ph.D. are each in political science with emphasis on international relations. Enrollment in the international relations program at the institution where he took his master's degree was unlimited; enrollment in the program at the university where he studied for the doctorate was small. He speaks highly of the latter because of the opportunity it provided for intimate faculty-student relationships, and is critical of the M.A. courses because of the large size of classes. He is now teaching courses in American government, public administration, and international organization, and is grateful for his undergraduate work in education as preparation for teaching. His evaluation of foreign language requirements is typical of many professors whose teaching loads preclude much research.

Present university requirements are ridiculous. They are merely obstacles to be passed by taking cram courses. Little to no working knowledge of the language is retained. Either require a mastery of one or two languages, or do away with the requirement entirely.

This respondent also had twenty hours of geography in undergraduate work, which he finds most useful in his present college teaching.

Respondent Number 6 has an undergraduate major in government with a minor in history. He took his M.A. in international relations, followed by a Ph.D. in political science with an emphasis on comparative government, concentrating especially on the government of Great Britain. After two years with a government agency he was employed by a small liberal arts college to inaugurate a group of new courses in political science and in international affairs. He teaches one course in government and another in international politics, and heads a social science division. He is critical of his doctoral studies in several respects.

Overspecialization is a mistake for teaching in a small liberal arts college. The seminars were so large in my graduate work that there was less opportunity for individual attention and discussion than I had expected. The principal weakness of my graduate training was an insufficient number of small seminars and group discussions. Likewise, I have found little use for foreign languages. Now concerned with the work of an entire division, my graduate training definitely did not have enough sociology, psychology and anthropology. The program for my M.A. and Ph.D. provided flexibility and opportunity for interdisciplinary study which I did not take advantage of. I regret it now.

He also adds that

Personality factors are very important, since the small college possesses the strengths and weaknesses of a family situation in many ways.

Respondent Number 7 majored in English and minored in economics for his bachelor's degree. He then obtained two master's degrees in international relations at different institutions. He is teaching a general course in social science, which includes political science, history, and international affairs. He rates his graduate study in international politics, political and social theory, and international law and organization as adequate preparation for his teaching, but would have welcomed more work in economics, the behavioral sciences, and geography. The courses in his graduate program which related to a specific geographic area he finds of little use for the over-all teaching of social science. He attributes the principal strength in his graduate training to excellent teaching. "To twist the old saw, one teacher of merit is worth a hundred books."

The undergraduate major of respondent Number 8 is economics with a minor in French. His M.A. and Ph.D. are each in political science with an emphasis on international relations. He studied for his graduate degrees in a department which did not permit much crossing of departmental lines. He is currently giving courses in local, state, and national government, as well as teaching one course in international politics and another in international organization. He evaluates his graduate training as more than adequate in the field of political science, but is critical of it for not providing greater opportunity for study in related fields. He particularly criticizes the teaching of international organization in his graduate program for confining itself to an examination of the structure of international organizations as opposed to a consideration of the problems with which international agencies deal.

The graduate study of respondent Number 9 was likewise in a university which did not permit much interdisciplinary effort. His undergraduate degree is in political science with no minor, and his master's and doctoral degrees are in political science with an emphasis on international relations. He finds this preparation adequate for the teaching he is doing in American and comparative government, but totally inadequate for the courses he gives in international relations.

The chief weakness of my training was the necessity to concentrate in the home department rather than have more general study of methodology in the social sciences.

Respondent Number 10 has an undergraduate major in economics and a minor in political science. He obtained a master's degree in political science and a Ph.D. in political science with an emphasis on international relations along with a minor in geography. He is now teaching general political science as well as one course in international relations and one in international organization. He also feels that broader training in the general social sciences would have been more useful to him. He is critical of the time and effort spent on the master's thesis and the doctoral dissertation as being disproportionate to the value he obtained.

The necessary research skills can be obtained by doing one thesis and the rest of the time would be better devoted to study or more class work.

He comments that his minor in geography has been especially helpful in his work.

Respondent Number 11 has an undergraduate major in education and a minor in social science. His M.A. and Ph.D. are both in the field of political science with an emphasis on international relations. However, most of the international relations emphasis consisted of courses in political science or history relating to a variety of areas of the world. He had no instruction in general international politics, international law and organization, or international economics. He reports that he feels at a great disadvantage now teaching survey courses in the social sciences.

My graduate work was too scattered and not based around any conceptual framework.

Respondent Number 12 obtained his bachelor's degree with a major in government and a minor in history, then a master's and a doctor's degree in international relations. He is at present teaching courses in European history and diplomatic history. He also served a number of years with a government agency.

I incline now to feel that . . . many graduate programs that I am acquainted with try to do two things which combine poorly. First, a regular academic program is offered based in most of its aspects upon traditional graduate studies. Second, an effort is made at professional preparation for government work. The fundamental purpose of the first kind of training is, it seems to me, to train the mind, to provide research skills, to educate teachers and to insure familiarity with traditional fields of study within each discipline. The purpose of the second kind of training is to provide useful information of a practical kind.

The two purposes, I think, are to some extent mutually exclusive.

On the basis of my experience, both in practical work in international affairs for the government and in the teaching field, I would be inclined to think that the two purposes ought to be separated into different kinds of institutions. A man might take a year or two in a regular graduate school with training in, say, economics, with minors in history or government, and then a shorter period of intensive study in techniques and information needed for a particular job.

International relations is *not* a discipline or a field of study. It does not have its own rules, idiom, procedure or tradition. It can never have them. It is made up by necessity of borrowings from economics, history, law, sociology, anthropology, military science, commerce, and foreign languages. It is I feel a mistake to mix these things up in a traditional academic framework.

Despite this criticism, he concludes:

. . . however I am not sure whether the hodgepodge of what is called international relations does not have some considerable advantages which outweigh or offset its serious disadvantages.

A number of persons included in the survey who had earned master's degrees in international relations are engaged in high school teaching. These respondents though trained as specialists, as defined in this report, are not practicing their specialty. However, most of them find graduate instruction in international relations useful for high school teaching.

Respondent Number 13 has an undergraduate major in political science, a minor in history, and an M.A. in international relations. She is teaching in a large high school giving five sections of a course in contemporary problems. She reports that her general work in international politics and international organization has been especially helpful to her. She regrets not having had some study in the behavioral sciences.

Respondent Number 14 has an undergraduate major in business, a minor in English, and a master's degree in international relations. The latter was taken under an interdepartmental committee. He finds his graduate training useful in teaching a course in civics and one in American history. The chief weakness of the committee arrangement under which he studied was its

failure to attempt to relate subjects one with the others and to establish over-all patterns into which individual subjects would fall.

Respondent Number 15 has an undergraduate major in history and an M.A. in international relations. He originally undertook graduate study with the idea of entering the Foreign Service. When he was not accepted by the Service, he took the necessary additional courses in education to obtain a secondary school teaching certificate. He finds his study of international relations to be especially useful in teaching world history.

Respondent Number 16 has an undergraduate major in history, a minor in education, and the master's degree in international relations. The purpose of his graduate study was to prepare for the Foreign Service. For a variety of reasons he did not attempt the Foreign Service examination and is teaching social studies in a large city school system. The social studies program emphasizes history, with considerable attention in the later stages given to problems in international affairs. "My graduate work in international relations has been extremely useful to me in my teaching."

One can see from the comments quoted above that graduates in international relations who become teachers are as critical of training programs for their failure to give attention to skills other than those of research and analysis as are the graduates who enter government service. The following comment is typical of the replies received from professors:

The major objective of graduate studies should be to develop abilities and skills. Ninety percent of what we know after graduation from graduate school is learned while engaged actively in teaching. No amount of graduate work can teach a man all that he will need to know during a professional career of some thirty to forty years. He learns most of it during his career.

Teachers who have come out of graduate programs in international relations where broad multidisciplinary study is permitted evaluate their graduate study as strong. Curricula which restrict a student to choosing most of his courses from the offerings of one department are regarded by students as being weak curricula. Teachers who have been trained in programs with limited enrollment praise this characteristic of their graduate institution, and graduates of programs where enrollment is unlimited tend to be critical of those programs for that reason.

Specialists Engaged in Other Occupations

It has been pointed out in the preceding chapter that government service and teaching are the principal vocational outlets for persons with graduate degrees in international relations. However, those in charge of specialized training programs in international relations profess to educate specialists for other careers, and international relationists are employed in many nongovernment and nonacademic pursuits. Therefore, the writer sought evaluations of graduate instruction from a great number of persons trained as specialists in international relations who are working in occupations other than teaching and government. Respondent Number 1 in this group has an undergraduate major in international relations as well as a master's degree in the field. He is employed by an oil company overseas as a government relations representative, acting as a liaison man between the company and local government officials and agencies. The respondent feels that his generalized training in international relations, which required study in the international aspects of political science, history, economics, the behavioral sciences, and geography, is of use to him in his job. He singles out as the chief strength of his graduate training the fact that he studied in a small institution where there were a rather sizable number of foreign students.

While a graduate student, I became well acquainted with the students from the country where I am now working. This experience aided my adjustment to this overseas environment.

Respondent Number 2 is also employed with an oil firm. He is living in the United States, however, and his position requires the analysis of financial and economic problems of foreign affiliates and foreign nations. His undergraduate major is in economics, and he has a two-year master's degree in international relations. He finds his graduate work in international relations useful for "the training it gave me in analysis of specific problems against a broad background of knowledge of the problem's general field." He is critical of his graduate study program because

too much time was required for lengthy written studies at the expense of more thought-provoking and less time-consuming, concise, written presentations.

Respondent Number 3 is also a finance analyst for an oil company. He has an undergraduate major in international relations with a minor in economics, and a master's degree in international relations. Although his duties consist largely of studying economic and balance payment trends for the company, he feels that his generalized instruction in international relations has been helpful to him in his present position.

There was heavy emphasis on international law and organization in my graduate work—a subject for which I have found no use. I could also have used more work in international economics and some business courses.

Respondent Number 4 has an undergraduate major in political science with a minor in English, and a master's degree in international relations. The latter was taken in a program which stressed diplomatic history. The respondent is the European representative for an American publishing firm, and his principal duty is to promote sales of the company's publications. He feels that the chief strength of his graduate training lay not in specific courses, but in the fact that the institution where he studied

brought together men and women from many countries and let them live together and study the same problems. I learned more about other people outside the classroom than inside and find that experience invaluable now that I constantly travel and mix with people from all countries in Europe. The principal weakness in my training was the complete absence of work in languages and geography. It was incredible to me that students should study about places they have no idea about or couldn't point to with accuracy on a map. Lack of languages will always be a major handicap in dealing on a business level or governmental level abroad. I find my knowledge of French, Greek and a little German making more friends and contacts for me than many months of speaking English could ever do. It is also embarrassing to find non-Americans in Europe speaking flawless English while Americans can hardly pronounce any other language than their mother tongue.

Respondent Number 5 has an undergraduate major in history, a minor in government, and a master's degree in international relations. He is employed by a bank, and one of his responsibilities is handling commercial business in foreign countries. He indicates that the generalized type of international relations training which he received has proved useful in his work. He feels that the strength and weakness of his graduate study both stem from the fact that he attended a small school. The strength—classes were small, giving plenty of opportunity for discussion; the weakness— very few persons outside the field of international relations have heard of the institution where he studied and

the lack of publicity operates against its graduates when seeking jobs in fields not directly related to governmental work.

Respondent Number 6 has an undergraduate degree in business and marketing, a master's degree in international relations, and a second M.A. in international economics. He prepared for work in the field of foreign trade from his undergraduate days and is traffic manager with the international division of a large corporation.

My M.A. in international relations has given me some general background for my job. However, my degree in international economics has been far more serviceable. The work I had in political theory and international law and organization has been of no general help whatsoever.

Respondent Number 7 with an undergraduate major in history and a minor in philosophy took his master's degree in international relations. He is working as a chartering broker's assistant, chartering vessels with cargoes of ores, grain, and coal from Africa and South America to the United States and Europe.

By far the chief strength of my general training in international relations was not the accumulation of knowledge, but rather the mental discipline developed and brought to bear in analyzing the many problems in the field. Let the layman accumulate facts; the specialist must be disciplined to analyze and interpret them.

He indicates that he lacks sufficient graduate study in economics for his present position.

Respondent Number 8 has an undergraduate major in international relations, a minor in English, and an M.A. in international relations. He is employed by Radio Free Europe in Europe. His chief duty is "to gather as much information as possible about the eastern European countries behind the iron curtain." The principal weakness of his training in light of his position is the lack of detailed knowledge of Central Europe. This could not have been foreseen since his career objectives were not clearly formed at the time of graduate study. He also feels the lack of good grounding in foreign languages. However,

general work in international politics, theory, organization, and history made me more aware and sensitive to the problems I encounter in my job. Personality factors are extremely important for anyone engaged in this kind of liaison work.

Respondent Number 9 who has an undergraduate degree in engineering, an M.A. in social work, another M.A. in political science, and a Ph.D. in international relations, is engaged in adult education activities in the field of world affairs. He reports the strength of his graduate training for his present position to be "its eclecticism and variety." He believes a broad knowledge of international affairs to be essential for adult education activities since a variety of problems are discussed in that kind of program.

One must also have desirable social personality traits if he is to deal with a broad group of professions and types of people.

Respondent Number 10 with an undergraduate major in chemical engineering and a minor in electrical engineering is studying for the Ph.D. in international relations while employed with the international relations department of a large scientific organization. His principal duties are of a public relations nature and his job also requires considerable report writing.

My international relations work gives me a basic understanding of the interrelationships between the political affairs of European nations and of the culture and background of these nations. This understanding is very important in my present job, especially as we deal with some thirty other nations. The main weakness of my training is that it is designed toward the attainment of a certain type of position and all other aspects are neglected, such as business and administrative training.

The graduate instruction does not permit the attaining of general skills that are necessary in most jobs. The Ph.D. requirements of most universities are fairly stringent. They do not allow much time to acquire a general background that may be essential in securing a future position. Ph.D.'s for the most part are usually granted to persons who will go into teaching rather than into business or government circles. This fact has led to a certain specialization, the defects of which are obvious. No time is permitted to acquire an understanding of public relations, sociology, psychology, and business methods and procedures that are so important in today's world.

Respondent Number 11 has an undergraduate major in political science and a minor in speech. His M.A. and Ph.D. are each in political science with an emphasis on international relations. He is employed by a private research agency which produces semi-popular materials on international affairs. The respondent feels that his study of international politics and political and social theory has been adequate. He is critical of his graduate work in international organization because

the course was devoted too much to the structure of international organizations and less to an analysis of the issues coming before these organizations. International law has been of no value to me in my present work. My history courses devoted too much time to European and American diplomacy to the neglect of Asia.

The respondent also believes that

more opportunity is needed for young graduate students to express their ideas in writing other than in the stultifying preparation of documented term papers. There should be more opportunity for the student to do thought pieces. The greatest strength of my graduate training was the broad nature of the field and training of the mind to sift the unimportant from the important and to stay with an issue until it has been clarified. The weaknesses in courses were those in which there was great emphasis on detail.

Respondent Number 12 has an undergraduate major in political science and a minor in Soviet area studies. His M.A. is in political science with an emphasis on international relations and his Ph.D. is in political science with an emphasis on the Soviet area. He holds a position with a private organization in Europe concerned with an analysis of the political trends in the Soviet area and publicizing those trends. Despite the fact that the respondent has had extensive area training and is employed as an area specialist, he wrote at length emphasizing the importance of the generalized training in international relations which he received.

Courses in political and social theory are especially important if only for purposes of conversation or as a part of the cultural training of an educated person in a European environment, and a familiarity with these subjects is vital. General education covering various disciplines is preferable to specialization if a choice is to be made. If there is time beyond generalized training to specialize, this is very desirable, but it should never be encouraged at the expense of general knowledge. I say this even though my present position seems to be a highly specialized one.

Respondent Number 13 has an undergraduate major in political science, a minor in journalism, and a master's degree in international relations. He is working on a daily paper, handling foreign and local copy. "All the work I did in international relations has been helpful to me in my present position." The reply of respondent Number 14, also a journalist, is just as terse. He has an undergraduate major in political science, a minor in economics, and an M.A. in international relations. He indicates that his graduate study provided excellent background for his job. He is critical of the work in history because

it concentrated on Europe and distorted the importance of that area as compared to other parts of the world.

Respondent Number 15 has an undergraduate major in political science, a minor in French, and a master's degree in international relations. He is associated with the state central committee of a major political party.

Although I am not working directly in international relations, the administration's foreign policy is a subject with which I deal constantly in working out programs for clubs and in editing speeches for some of our candidates.

Respondent Number 16 has an undergraduate major in political science, a minor in economics, and a two-year master's degree in international relations. His graduate program did not require a thesis and was one which emphasized small group discussions, and writing numerous but brief papers. The respondent is serving as an assistant to a United States congressman. He feels that his graduate study has been extremely useful to him.

For my job there would have been no substitute for the broad character of the graduate program in which I studied with its emphasis upon training the generalist.

Summary

One hundred fifty-two graduates of specialized training programs in international relations were queried during the preparation of this report. Each was asked to evaluate his graduate instruction in light of the kind of work in which he is now engaged. Excerpts from the replies of about one third of the respondents have been quoted in this chapter to show what the "products" of specialized training programs believe the principal strengths and weaknesses of specialized training in international relations to be. Specialists now engaged in government work or teaching tend to regard broad generalized education in international relations as useful preparation for those professions. In general, specialists in nongovernment and nonacademic pursuits have somewhat less praise for training in international relations as preparation for a career. Most graduates, irrespective of their occupations, are critical of graduate instruction for its failure to provide training to develop skills other than research and analysis and for the lack of concern about the personality traits required in a specialist. Graduates of international relations curricula have considerable criticism of the nature of foreign language requirements for graduate degrees, and most specialists do not rate as useful the exercise of writing the type of doctoral dissertation now required by most doctoral programs in international relations.

CHAPTER 5

Some Suggestions for Strengthening Specialized Training Programs

SPECIALIZED TRAINING in international relations as now conducted in graduate schools in American colleges and universities has been described and evaluated in the preceding chapters. The description and evaluation were based on a survey of producers—those persons vested with the responsibility for international relations curricula in institutions of higher education; consumers—those individuals who employ international relationists; and products—those persons who once engaged in graduate study of international relations and who now hold positions as specialists. Thus far in this volume the writer has confined himself largely to presenting the observations of others and to making generalizations arrived at as a result of his survey of representative producers, consumers, and products. This final brief chapter contains certain suggestions for the improvement of graduate instruction in international relations. The suggestions are those which the writer believes to be warranted by the data in the foregoing chapters. Persons who have read the preceding pages may well derive a different set of conclusions from the material presented. This chapter summarizes the suggestions of many producers, consumers, and products as to ways and means for strengthening graduate instruction in international relations, but the summary is colored by the fact that it contains only those suggestions to which the writer subscribes.

Courses in the Graduate Curriculum

The study of international relations is designed to develop in a candidate for a graduate degree an understanding of what causes states to project themselves beyond their borders, how states attempt to achieve their foreign policy objectives, and why they succeed or fail in the quest. This understanding cannot be found in the study of any one discipline. Nearly every problem in international affairs has political, economic, and social aspects which affect not just one or two nations, but many nations. Most foreign policy decisions involve policy-makers in questions of power, ethics, and ideology. The general knowledge needed to comprehend the complexities of international affairs seems to be limitless, and the specific knowledge required to analyze problems differs from problem to problem. Therefore, international relations is of necessity a multidisciplinary field of study and no series of courses can be designated as the ideal program for training specialists.

The efforts of educators over the past thirty-five years to make international relations manageable as a field of graduate study have shown that basic courses in international politics, international organization, diplomatic history, international economics, and international law constitute a sound core of courses around which to build a graduate study program. Training would be strengthened by the inclusion of more materials from economics, geography, and the behavioral sciences in the basic core of courses. These materials could be incorporated into curricula in one of two ways. Teachers of international relations could themselves include more materials from economics, geography, and the behavioral sciences in courses in international politics, international organization, and diplomatic history. Or, relevant departments could be requested to prepare special courses in economics and geography and the behavioral sciences geared to the needs of students of foreign policy.

The career for which the student is preparing provides the most desirable guide for selecting those courses which he takes in addition to the basic core of courses in the international relations curriculum. The complexities of foreign policy indicate that the best interests of the student are served when the selection of his courses is not limited by departmental lines. If the objective of a program is to train a person in political science or in economics or to develop some other functional specialty, then there is merit in restricting the student to a selection of courses from the offerings of a single department.

When the courses for any student's graduate study program in international relations have been chosen, there remains the fundamental task of integration. Diverse courses should be harmonized; the materials from many disciplines must be related so that they have meaning as a whole rather than as a sum of fragmented parts. A number of devices which have proved relatively successful as integrators for multidisciplinary study have been described in chapter 2. Graduate instruction in international relations will be strengthened materially as faculties increase their efforts to integrate the diverse courses which constitute the curricula of specialized training programs.

Skills

A principal weakness of graduate instruction in international relations in many institutions is that insufficient attention is given to the development of skills other than research and analysis. Virtually every occupation for which the international relationist is trained demands that the specialist possess a relatively high degree of skill in written and oral expression. Students preparing for careers in government service in particular are better served by exercises requiring the preparation of numerous, concise, clearly and logically written reports than by preparation of a few lengthy and carefully documented seminar papers. Courses requiring students to present materials orally, to engage in cooperative research, and to participate in group discussion of problems of foreign policy are relatively more successful in developing the range of skills which government requires of its employees than are courses conducted by the traditional lecture–examination–term paper method.

Training programs designed to prepare students for academic careers could be strengthened if more were done to develop those skills required of a good teacher. There exists an unfortunate but widespread antipathy between departments of education and other departments in many universities. The removal of this barrier is worthy of the most intensive efforts of parties on both sides of this academic fence. Special courses or projects developed cooperatively by representatives of the education and international relations curricula and designed to transmit to the student of world affairs some of the elements of good teaching without the necessity of majoring in education are not out of the realm of possibility. The difficulties are many but the potential rewards for the student are so great that this proposal merits the most serious consideration.

Many graduate students in international relations hope for employment in fields other than government service and teaching. Adequate preparation for nongovernmental and nonacademic pursuits also requires the inauguration of courses, projects, and assignments constructed to develop skills other than those of research and analysis. The program at Western Reserve University has been outlined in chapter 3 to illustrate what can be done to combine education in international relations with training designed to develop the skills required in adult education. The principle underlying that program suggests other types of activity which might be developed. For example, seminars taught jointly by professors of international relations and professors of communication arts might be useful in training students preparing for careers in radio, television, and newspaper journalism. The student's work in such a course might consist of the preparation of papers on foreign policy problems in the form of newspaper articles and radio and television scripts. His work would be criticized for content by the professors of international relations and for writing techniques by the professors of communication arts.

The degree of skill in the use of foreign languages now required by institutions offering specialized training in international relations is a source of dissatisfaction with most graduates of training programs and with most employers. The present unsatisfactory state of affairs might be resolved if the career objectives of any student were made the basis for determining the degree of skill to be acquired.

The student who seeks a career which will necessitate a sojourn abroad should acquire the ability to read, write, and speak at least one foreign language with some fluency. The student whose career will demand that he engage in research should be required to develop considerable skill in reading one or more foreign languages relevant to his field of interest. Students who do not plan to engage in research and whose future employment will be in the United States could devote time during their graduate study to more useful endeavors than developing skill in the use of a foreign language. Whenever knowledge of a foreign language is a requirement for a graduate degree, the requirement should be for skill in the use of the language and not just a requirement of tradition which may be met if the student acquires a smattering of knowledge enabling him to pass a superficial examination in the language.

Organization of Graduate Study

The type of organization used in conducting training in international relations does not materially affect the quality of instruction. The advantages and disadvantages of the principal types of organization—the special school or department of international relations, the interdepartmental committee, or organization of the work within the department of political science were pointed out in chapter 1. It was emphasized there that none of the advantages and disadvantages of any type of organization is inherent. In practice, the principal advantage of the separate school or department has been that instructors have more time to devote to students of international relations and have been permitted greater freedom to construct special courses to meet the needs of the international relationist. The same end can be achieved under the interdepartmental committee or within the department of political science if some one person who is given prime responsibility for the international relations curriculum devotes all his time to that curriculum. Each university can formulate its policy with regard to organizing study only in light of its own peculiar resources and problems.

Length of Study

It seems to the writer that the most satisfactory way to differentiate among the purposes of specialized training programs would be to reserve the one-year master's degree in international relations for the student whose career objectives are not well defined, the two-year M.A. in international relations for those preparing for nonacademic work, and the Ph.D. in political science with emphasis on international relations as well as the Ph.D. in international relations *per se* for those going into teaching. Obviously, the difficulties of conducting a satisfactory training program in as broad a field as international relations are compounded in the case of those programs which require only a year to complete. This fact would seem to indicate that only superior students should be permitted to enroll in one-year study programs if the general objectives of training in international relations are to be achieved in that brief period of time. Nevertheless, generally speaking, the current admission requirements for one-year programs are less stringent than those for two-year programs, and in both cases the requirements for admission appear to be insufficiently high.

Requirements for Admission

It would be most desirable if every institution would screen all applicants for admission to graduate study in international relations carefully and strictly limit the number of students admitted. During one, two, or three years of graduate instruction even the best students achieve only a partial understanding of the complex interrelationships of many disciplines as applied to the study of foreign policy problems. The student with an undergraduate record slightly better than the average finds it difficult indeed to attain a desirable degree of mastery of the broad and somewhat amorphous field of international relations. The multidisciplinary nature of international relations suggests not only that enrollment for graduate training in this field be limited to students with outstanding academic records but also that admission be confined to those with a broad undergraduate education in the liberal arts.

Specialized training programs in international relations would be strengthened further if the personality traits of applicants for admission were assessed along with their academic records. Most graduate instructors in international relations are not equipped nor do they have the time to correct the personality deficiencies of students. Yet a major criticism of the products of international relations curricula is that too frequently they lack flexibility, sensitivity, capacity to endure frustration, and a variety of other personality traits which employers deem essential for careers in international relations. This weakness can be corrected in part by a stricter admissions policy.

Short of giving every applicant a Rorschach test or conducting a personal interview with him before admission, properly devised application blanks have been used with considerable success by some institutions to obtain an idea of the personality of the applicant for admission. One can infer much about a person from a written statement as to why he wishes to undertake graduate instruction in international relations. A story, perhaps untrue, was told about the selection of personnel for duty in the tropics and the Arctic during World War II. The whole gamut of psychological tests was administered to each officer. A brief questionnaire was also employed that included an item on his preference for one or the other climate. The only item that correlated with later performance was the preference item. "One can infer much about a person by letting him tell what he likes, what moves him to action, and what he is like."[1]

The type and extent of the applicant's extracurricular activities suggest his leadership qualities. The kinds of recreation in which he engages provide a hint as to his resourcefulness. Questions such as these have long been used by universities in addition to letters of recommendation to assess the whole person of applicants for fellowships. They are just as useful for a training program which wishes to consider more than academic record as a basis for admission.

The number of students admitted to graduate instruction in international relations would be curtailed automatically if enrollment were restricted to students having outstanding academic records, broad education in the liberal arts, and superior personal qualities. In addition, training programs would be strengthened if institutions would limit enrollments to the number which would permit the teaching of the basic core of courses in the international relations curriculum in small classes. Satisfactory instruction in so complex a field of study requires that ample opportunity be provided for thorough discussion among students and professors.

Conclusion

The United States faces an awesome responsibility in the conduct of its foreign policy. The maintenance of peace or, if war should come, then the winning of that war, is dependent in great measure upon how effectively the United States carries out its political, economic, military, technical, information, and cultural programs in countries all over the world, as well as on the policies it follows in dozens of international organizations and agencies. Peace or the successful waging of armed conflict does not

[1] M. B. Smith, J. S. Bruner, and R. W. White, *Opinions and Personalities* (New York: John Wiley & Sons, 1956), p. 281.

hinge on governmental action alone. Each is contingent on the conduct of American business and the activities of other groups overseas. Each depends on the degree of understanding of international problems possessed by the electorate. This understanding, in turn, requires good teaching in schools at all levels, effective adult education programs, knowledgeable reporting and interpretation of events and trends by newspapers, magazines, radio, and television, and depends on the effectiveness of the activities of hundreds of private agencies interested in world affairs.

It is apparent that there exists a need for persons with a diversity of training, possessing a wide range of factual knowledge and many different skills in numerous occupations and endeavors. The requirements range from the generalist—the broadly and liberally educated man—on one hand, to the most narrowly trained subject-matter expert or technician on the other. Between these two extremes on the continuum of needs is the specialist in international relations.

The training of this specialist is narrower than that of the generalist in that his education in numerous disciplines is focused on one aspect of the problems of man, the international one. Yet the training is considerably broader than that given to the technician or the person educated in one discipline, and thus moves against the current of graduate instruction in American colleges and universities which is toward narrower and narrower specialization. The reasons for the trend toward narrower specialization were well stated by the Commission on Human Resources and Advanced Training:

Specialization breeds more specialization. . . . The automobile created the need for experts in traffic control. Aeroplane travel created a need for long-range weather forecasting of greater accuracy than had been considered necessary before, and in the process increased the demand for meteorologists and meteorological research. . . . With the growth of industry financial problems became more complex and increased the demands for accountants, tax experts, specialists on foreign trade, and economic experts of other kinds. Simultaneously there grew up a monetary exchange system of clearing houses and bank credit flowing smoothly through the increasingly complex network of commerce and industry.

In another sense also specialization begets further specialization. The sheer increase in the amount of knowledge causes one field of specialization to break up into even more specialized areas. . . . As knowledge has increased in the past, the number of new fields of specialization has grown; as knowledge will continue to increase in the future, even newer fields of specialization will emerge.[2]

Graduate training in international relations is designed to reduce the distortion which is inevitable in overspecialization, while at the same time giving focus to broader education. The quality of the product of graduate training programs in international relations has been constantly improving. It will continue to improve and the market for specialists will constantly expand if institutions giving graduate instruction in international relations concentrate their efforts on thorough training of carefully selected students. The student, the graduate institution, and the nation will be better served as the quality of training programs improves.

[2] Dael Wolfle, *America's Resources of Specialized Talent* (New York: Harper & Bros., 1954), pp. 2–3.

INDEX

Ability, general, Foreign Service test of, 51–52

Academic record, as basis for admission to international relations programs, 124

Adjustment to foreign environment, 45

Administrative ability, need for training in, 51, 114

Admission requirements, suggestions for strengthening, 123–24

Advanced Comparative Government, 83

Africa, area study programs on, 16

Alaska, 5

Allies, 8

American Council on Education, v, viii, 52

American diplomatic history, 79

American Institutions and Issues of Public Policy, 73

Analysis of Policy and Power, 76

Anthropology, as factor in international relations, 7

Approaches and Methods in the Study of International Relations, as example of interdisciplinary approach, 73–74

Approaches to teaching international relations, 19–21

Arctic, 124

Area course, as single integrative course, 37

Area study programs, 15–18
  criteria for, 17
  as "laboratory example," 67
  multidisciplinary character of, 16–17, 18
  number of, 16
  as preparation for teaching in the social sciences, 106
  as strength in international relations program, 97

Armed Forces, view of members of, on training in international relations, 98–99

Army Specialized Training Programs, 16

Asia, 74
  neglect of, in history programs, 115

Atlantic and Pacific Oceans as factors in international relations, 5

Background, general, Foreign Service test of, 51–52

Basic Factors in World Politics, 66, 68

Behavioral sciences in international relations programs
  inadequate instruction in, 32, 33–35, 95, 100, 102, 106, 115
  suggestions for inclusion of more materials on, 119

Berlitz Language Schools, 62

British Empire, 6

Broad view of foreign policy problems as strength of international relations program, 92–96, 99, 102, 115–17

Bryant Professor of Geography and International Relations, 73

Career objectives and selection of courses, 119–20

Careers for specialist in international relations, 56–62

Carnegie Endowment for International Peace, v, vii, viii, xi, 75

Carr, E. H., 38

Central Europe, 114

Central Europe in World Affairs, 79

Central Intelligence Agency, xi
  career opportunities in, for international relationists, 60

128

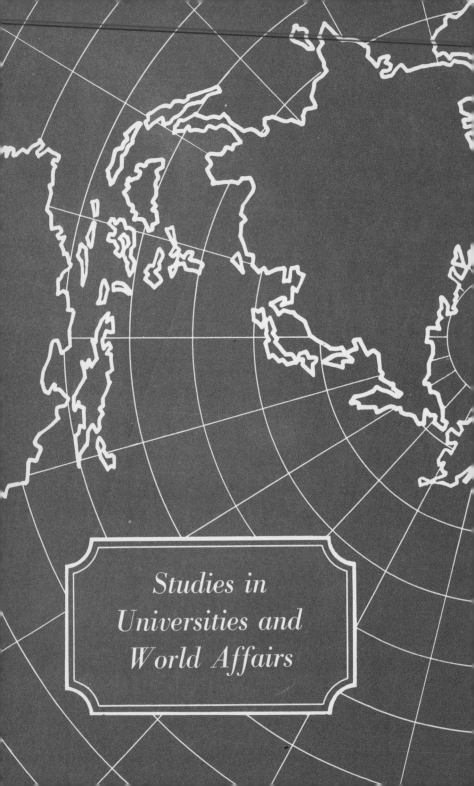

Studies in
Universities and
World Affairs